Abhandlungen zur Kunst-,Musik-und
Literaturwissenschaft, Band 258

On Imitation, Imagination and Beauty

A Critical Reassessment of the Concept of the Literary Artist During the Early German "Aufklärung"

by Steven D. Martinson

1977

Bouvier Verlag Herbert Grundmann · Bonn

Dedicated to my parents.

CIP-Kurztitelaufnahme der Deutschen Bibliothek
MARTINSON, STEVEN D.
On imitation, imagination and beauty: a critical reassessment of the concept of the literary artist during the early German "Aufklärung". - 1. Aufl. - Bonn: Bouvier, 1977.
(Abhandlungen zur Kunst-, Musik- und Literaturwissenschaft; Bd. 258)
ISBN 3-416-01406-5
ISSN 0567-4999

Dasjenige aber nur allein ist
fruchtbar, was der Einbildungskraft
freies Spiel lässt (Lessing, Laokoon).

Acknowledgments

An expression of thanks is certainly in order to those people who assisted, either directly or indirectly, to the completion of this study.

To my grandparents, Rev. and Mrs. Theodore and Marie Brackman, to my parents, Mr. and Mrs. R. Del and Ruth Martinson, and to my understanding wife, Elizabeth, I owe a debt of thanks for their encouragement and unfailing support.

I am likewise indebted to Professor Gunter H. Hertling, the chairman of the supervisory committee, for his generous assistance and expert direction of the dissertation. Professor Ernst Behler and William H. Rey were an inspiration to me and I thank them for their helpful suggestions. Thanks also to Dr. M. S. South, whose Lessing seminar confirmed my interest in the Aufklärung.

Further thanks are extended to Dr. Sabine Solf and Frau Degen for their kind assistance while in Wolfenbüttel in the summer of 1976.

Sole responsibility, of course, for the contents of this study is borne by the author himself.

Seattle, Washington

May, 1977

TABLE OF CONTENTS

Textual Note

We quote from the actual 18th Century works and
reliable reprints, and make use of the earliest editions
available. All of the primary literature cited is from the
Herzog August Bibliothek in Wolfenbüttel, the Niedersächsische
Landesbibliothek-Göttingen, and the Suzallo Library of the
University of Washington. We have indicated in the footnotes
which copy was used in the hope of assisting others in locat-
ing these valuable materials.

Every attempt was made to preserve the original spelling
and punctuation. For the sake of consistency, however, a
number of changes were necessary. Corrections, marked by
bracket notation ([]), were made on the basis of what was
correct at that time. Since the use of ß was not used con-
sistently as a convention, we have used -ss- everywhere. We
also used the comma, where in many 18th Century texts the
virgula (/) was employed. The designation (") represents
"Umlaut". A single hyphen (-) is used where most of the
texts employ =. 18th Century fractura is replaced by 20th
Century roman script, and italics, unless otherwise indicated, represent italics in the original texts.

INTRODUCTION

THE GERMAN AUFKLÄRUNG AND THE
SEARCH FOR SYNTHESIS

> To understand, not the antithesis
> of classicism and romanticism,
> but their synthesis, is the way
> progress lies (John G. Robertson).[1]

To speak of a "German Enlightenment" as an historical
occurence is to convey the false impression that this phase of
Germany's intellectual history was nationally autonomous. It
was not. But neither was it as dependent upon foreign influ-
ences as Nicolas Monsiaux's famous drawing (ca. 1795) of
Voltaire and Frederick "The Great"--the depiction of the
philosopher-critic instructing his pupil--suggests.[2] The
uniqueness of the German Aufklärung is found in the inter-
action between the enlightened ideas of French, English and
Italian philosophes and the troublesome questions of the
German Aufklärer concerning the problem, first discernible in
Leibniz's monadology, of man's ultimate perfectibility.[3]

There exists a persistent and now conventional dissec-
tion of Germany's intellectual history into neat, albeit
immediately comprehensible categories. An ominous rift between the Aufklärung and the ensuing movement of Sturm und
Drang is thus postulated and German classicism and romanticism are viewed as mortal enemies.[4]

New Directions

Although there were a few interpreters of 18th Century Germany who remained somewhat discontent with such radical dichotomizing (most notably, John G. Robertson and Friedrich J. Schneider)[5], it was not until approximately the mid-1960's that an "Umwertung und Neubewertung des Aufklärungszeitalters" (Adam Wandruszka)[6] began to take place.

In 1963, Janine Beunzod persuasively argued that the Sturm und Drang movement did not constitute a break with the Aufklärung.[7] In the introduction to his anthology of selected texts from the time of the Aufklärung, Gerhard Funke (1963) pointed out further continuity within 18th Century Germany by accentuating the united respect for the Socratic method among writers of apparently diverse philosophical and literary orientation.[8] What Buenzod had done for Aufklärung and Sturm und Drang, Helmut Schanze (1966) did for German romanticism. Schanze's enlightening book[9], rejects Georg Lukács' claim (among others) that German romanticism constitutes a radical "Bruch mit der Aufklärung"[10], and thus uncovers the basic continuity between the two movements.

Among Marxist interpretations of the time, Werner Krauss' studies (1963) have continued to be highly influential in the overall reevaluation of the Aufklärung.[11] And, from a philosophical perspective, Max Horkheimer's and Theodor Adorno's postulation of the dialectic of the Enlightenment and its inherent self-destructiveness (consistent with their concept of negative dialectics) has been particularly instrumental in motivating the recent reassessments of the Aufklärung.[12]

Among American historians, Peter Gay's award-winning interpretation (1966) of the Enlightenment was a milestone on the road to a far more veracious account of the time.[13] And Peter Hanns Reill (1975) finally laid to rest the all-too prevalent notion that the Enlightenment was essentially non-historical in outlook and scope.[14]

The "Age of Enlightenment" is no longer perceived as constituting what Thomas Paine first termed an "Age of Reason".[15] This notion is simply not born out by fact. Reason and emotion coexist and dialectically complement one another from the very inception of the movement.[16] In its philosophical manifesta-tion, the German Aufklärung may be interpreted as an ongoing attempt to reconcile what is essentially Cartesian rationalism with the empiricism of Locke and Hume.[17] This is especially pronounced in Moses Mendelssohn's Briefe über die Empfindungen (1755), written at the height of the Aufklärung, and is first visible in Leibniz's theory of the monad (1714, publ. 1720).[18] The psychological foundation of the aesthetic theory of the time is manifested in Moses Mendelssohn's attempt to unite the higher ("obere") with the lower ("untere") powers of the soul ("Seelenkräfte")--a distinction which represents an inter-nationalization of Baumgarten's differentiation between the higher and lower faculty of knowledge ("Erkenntnisvermögen") and which serves as a prelude to Schiller's vision of a synthesis of the same after the aesthetic education of man.[19]

Although some critics have been reluctant to incorporate the spread of pietism and Empfindsamkeit (the secular form of

pietism) under the heading of Aufklärung[20], only in so doing
will a more accurate account of the time be won. As Gerhard
Sauder has persuasively argued, even the pietists themselves
sought to unite reason and feeling.[21] To assume, then, as
many have done, that there was an antagonism between reason
and emotion at the time of the Aufklärung, is to misrepresent
the facts. In order to properly understand the Aufklärung, we
must desist from associating it merely with Rationalismus[22],
and begin to comprehend that this period in Germany's intellectual history, like that of other periods, reflects a search
for synthesis in the uniting of reason and emotion.

The German Aufklärung is a time of critical evaluation.
It is a time of the gradual dismantling of the adornments of
the Baroque. And it is a time which points to an age to come,
to an Age of Reason, as Isaak Iselin prophesied in his
Geschichte der Menschheit (1764).[23] The "Age of Enlightenment"
as an historical occurrence did not embody true enlightenment.
Nor did its chief representatives ever claim to have achieved
it. Similar in tone to Novalis's call for a golden age to
come at the end of Die Christenheit oder Europa (1799, publ.
1826)[24], the historical age of Aufklärung ends with the almost
Laokoonian cry of Gotthold Ephraim Lessing in Die Erziehung
des Menschengeschlechts (1780): "...sie wird kommen, sie wird
gewiss kommen, die Zeit der Vollendung..."[25] It is this projection into the future which characterizes the historical
vision of the German Aufklärung.

The Ideal and the Crisis

If one may speak of a common ideal among Aufklärer, then it most certainly must be that of the vision of harmony between reason and emotion within man and the resultant blending of man with society. In the literature of the time, Wieland's Agathon stands as the most representative example of this ideal of the Aufklärung. Agathon, the truly enlightened individual, attains unity of mind and body only after having informed reason with emotion and having tempered emotion with reason.[26] And it is this ideal of harmony which unites the Aufklärung with German classicism.[27]

Curiously enough, however, it is also in Agathon that we learn of the ultimate unattainability of this ideal of human perfection.[28] This revealing admission points to what we understand to be the crisis of the German Aufklärung. This crisis consists in the rather shocking confession that the power of the will is oftentimes stronger than that of reason, and that this is so because the will requires less time to react than reason does to reflect. For Breitinger, it was "ausser allem Zweifel, dass das Temperament und die ausgelassenen Triebe unseres Willens offt stärcker und ungestumer sind, als die Vernunft"[29]. Johann Elias Schlegel openly admits:

> ...dass unser Verstand sich allemal nach den
> Einfällen unserer Begierden richtet, dass er
> für recht hält, was er zuvor gut geheissen;
> und dass er allezeit bey unsern Leidenschaften
> das Amt dererjenigen vertritt, welche entweder
> aus Ueberzeugung oder aus Schuldigkeit die
> gründliche Ursache zum Vorschein bringen müssen,
> um die Unternehmungen ihrer Herren zu recht-
> fertigen.[30]

And Moses Mendelssohn first reveals that this is so because

the will is more immediate than reason:

> Die sinnliche Erkenntnis kann gleichfalls
> mächtiger werden als die Vernunft, 1) durch
> die Menge der Merkmale, die wir wahrnehmen,
> 2) durch ihre beständige Gegenwart, und 3)
> durch die Geschwindigkeit, mit welcher wir
> uns alles das Gute vorstellen, das in einer
> sinnlichen Erkenntniss enthalten ist.[31]

The same thought is again voiced by Schiller in his dissertation, entitled Versuch über den Zusammenhang der tierischen
Natur des Menschen mit seiner Geistigen (1780), where he maintains that:

> ...die tierische Empfindungen mit unwider-
> stehlicher und gleichsam tyrannischer Macht
> die Seele zu Leidenschaften und Handlungen
> fortreissen und über die geistigsten selbst
> nicht selten die Oberhand bekommen.[32]

The crisis of the Aufklärung is thus rooted in the knowledge
that the impulsiveness of the will is able to subvert, time
and again, the dictates of reason. And it is precisely this
sensitivity toward time which informs the realistic-deter-
ministic vision of the Aufklärung.

The so-called optimism of the Aufklärer, then, is in
need of reassessment. For the Aufklärer were acutely aware
of the fleeting nature of their ideal. That is why they
spoke of that golden age of harmonious perfection, not as if it
had been made manifest among them, but in terms of its ultimate
inaccessibility.

This is implied already from the generally accepted idea
of man as part animal and part angel, or god. In the Second
Book of Über den Ursprung des Übels (1734), Albrecht von
Haller defines man as a "zweideutig Mittelding von Engeln und

von Vieh".[33] This view of man appears again in Wieland's

Agathon. Although Wieland's hero remains convinced that one

must strive for ever greater wisdom and virtue, he nonetheless

admits:

> Dass der Mensch-auf der einen Seite den Tieren
> des Feldes, auf der andern den höhern Wesen und
> der Gottheit selber verwandt-zwar eben so
> unfähig sei, ein blosses Tier als ein blosser
> Geist zu sein;...[34]

And once again, in Schiller's discussion of "Tierische

Empfindungen" in his dissertation, there is the insight, "dass

er [man] das unselige Mittelding von Vieh und Engel ist".[35]

It is precisely this admission that man is half animal which

keeps him from attaining any god-like perfection.

An unforgettable image of this crisis is to be found in

Mendelssohn's Briefe über die Empfindungen, in Euphranor's

description of his father's painting of a sinking ship. In his

attempt to persuade Theokles, the older man of reason, of the

power of emotion, the young sensualist builds up the following

image:

> Du selbst, Theokles! wie oft hat dich das
> Gemählde ergötzt, das in dem Cabinette
> meines Vaters, nicht weit vom Eingange,
> pranget? Es ist ein Schiff, das lange
> genug, mit Sturm und Wellen gekämpft, und
> endlich untergeht. Noch versucht das
> arbeitsame Schiffsvolk seine letzten
> Kräfte. Sie stehen, vom weissen Schaume
> der Wellen bedeckt, und frischen sich
> einander zur Arbeit an. Aber umsonst:
> Jetzt führt der Sturm eine hochgethürmte
> Welle auf sie los, die ihnen den gewissen
> Tod bringt. Sie sehen es, erblassen, und
> die vergeblichen Ruder sinken aus ihren
> matten Händen (Werke, p. 395).

The ideal of the German Aufklärer was shattered on the rock of reality. Deep within the human soul, as Mendelssohn informs us, a war rages between opposing forces (Rhapsodie, Werke, p. 456), the very forces which set our soul into motion. But this battle of conflicting interests among the various motives of the soul ("Triebfeder der Seele"), those dark compulsions ("dunkle Neigungen"), is actually carried on unconsciously, without the soul itself even being aware of the struggle:

> Alles dieses kann von selbst, vermöge der
> Natur unserer Seele, in dem Gemüthe
> vorgehen, ohne dass sich die Seele nothwendig
> dieser gegenseitigen Berechnung bewusst
> seyn musste (Werke, p. 456).

The most, then, that the soul is able to do is to carry out the wishes of an impulse which has overpowered the faculty of desire ("das Begehrungsvermögen"):

> Sie [die Seele] fühlt einen Trieb, etwas zu
> thun, oder zu lassen, sie fühlt auch den
> Widerstand der entgegengesetzten Begierden
> und Verabscheuungen, und entschliesst sich,
> das zu thun, wozu sie den mächtigsten Reiz
> verspürt (Werke, p. 456).

Even the use of the verb, verspüren, "to become aware of", reveals the unconscious nature of these "dunkle Neigungen".

> Daher sind die Affecte und die sinnlichen
> Empfindungen so oft mächtiger als die
> Vernunft (Werke, p. 458).

In the final analysis, then, it is emotion, not reason, which commands.

Poetics and Aesthetics

In the poetics and aesthetics[36] of early 18th Century Germany, the struggle for synthesis is particularly obvious in the ongoing attempt to mediate between extremes, by informing

reason with imagination and tempering the creative imagination with reason. Indeed, as we endeavor to illustrate, the
principles which underly and inform the poetic and aesthetic
theory of the early Aufklärung, in particular, prove to be of
immense consequence for the development of modern German literature. It is with this pre-Lessing phase of the German
Aufklärung that the present study is concerned.

Although some significant advances in this area have been
made[37], a more general, critical reevaluation of the poetic
and aesthetic theory of Johann Christoph Gottsched, Johann
Jacob Bodmer, Johann Jacob Breitinger, Johann Elias Schlegel,
and other representatives of the early Aufklärung, in light of
the more general reassessment of the Enlightenment in general,
has not been attempted. It is our purpose to critically re-
assess the poetic and aesthetic thought of the period 1721-
1751, i.e. from the appearance of the Discourse der Mahlern by
Bodmer and Breitinger to that of the fourth and last edition
of Gottsched's Versuch einer Critischen Dichtkunst vor die
Deutschen. It was not until 1755, with the appearance of
Lessing's Miss Sara Sampson, Mendelssohn's Briefe über die
Empfindungen, Nicolai's Briefe über den jetzigen Zustand der
schönen Künste und Wissenschaften, and, interestingly enough,
Kant's dissertation, De igne, that the German Aufklärung
reached its height. In our study, we include the most popular
and influential periodicals of this period only insofar as
they contribute to the dissemination of these theories.

References to the main theoreticians on aesthetics during
this time (Alexander Baumgarten, Georg Friedrich Meier, Moses
Mendelssohn and Johann Sulzer) will also be included.

In order to limit the scope of the present study, however,
we will concentrate primarily on the main works of this period
which deal with the problems of imitation, imagination, taste,
beauty, and the sublime. We are of the considered opinion that
these early enlightened critics, and artists in their own
right, consciously strove to maintain what we later term the
golden mean in the creation of literary works of art. In
order for literature to be genuinely effective, these early
Aufklärer encouraged the maintenance of a balance between
verisimilitude and creative freedom in the imitation of
nature, poetic enthusiasm and controlled expression in the
workings of the creative imagination, and sensation and
understanding in the exercise of good Taste. Only in light of
this struggle for synthesis can the poetics and aesthetics of
the early Aufklärung be properly understood.

With respect to methodology, we are not of the opinion
that the history of ideas reflects a natural and logical progression. Unlike advocates of Geistesgeschichte, we simply
do not believe in the Geist within which the thought of all
individual writers is mysteriously consumed. Such a procedure
almost always leads to abstractions which no longer reflect
factual authenticity.

Alfred Baeumler, for example, expressly speaks of the

"need" to interpret the history of 18th Century German aesthetics from the viewpoint of Kant's ·Kritik der Urteils-kraft.[38] The course of poetic and aesthetic thought in 18th Century Germany is said to culminate, logically and neces-sarily, in Kant's work on aesthetic judgment. It is therefore no surprise that writers like Johann Ulrich König, who con-sulted the French (and others) in matters of Taste, should fare so poorly in Baeumler's account.

Now to our mind, such an approach encourages the reading of history in the exact reverse of its actual development. To impose our perspectives and expectations on any period of history is simply to obscure our vision. No period in history can be properly understood unless we first go to the sources and from there allow the writers and artists of that time to speak to us.

We do not wish to suggest, however, that certain periods and individual writers develop in a vacuum. That is why we remain sensitive toward the differences which separate the work of the early Aufklärer, while, at the same time, looking for continuity.

Liscow's, Pyra's, and Meier's rejection of Gottsched and his Circle[39], Lessing's polemical condemnation of Gottsched in the 17. Literaturbrief (1759)[40], Goethe's terse dismissal of the poetics of that time in Dichtung und Wahrheit (1811/1814)[41], and the numerous accounts of the early Aufklärung by late 19th and early 20th Century scholars[42], have been directly responsible for the all-too prevalent trend to dismiss the poetic and aesthetic thought of the pre-Lessing phase of the Aufklärung as essentially unimaginative and ultimately barren.

On the contrary, the early Aufklärer were highly industrious in their endeavor to establish for Germany a nationally autonomous literature based upon a thorough knowledge of the German language. There is, of course, disagreement on the direction which the Aufklärung should pursue. And yet, there is commonality precisely in this disagreement. For what unites the German Aufklärer is criticism, the very impetus for debate.

For these early enlightened critics, literary criticism was perceived as science. The literary critic was to remain dispassionate and was expected to prove his statements on the basis of convincing evidence in accordance with the accepted rules of art. In his introduction to Bodmer's Critische Betrachtungen über die Poetischen Gemählde der Dichter of 1741, Breitinger addresses himself to the "Amt eines rechtschaffenen Critici" and to the "unerkannte Nutzbarkeit der Critischen Freyheit".[43] The genuine critic is here defined as "eine Person, die Lob und Tadel nach Verdienen ausspendet" (BPG, p. 2*) and within whom "Verstand und Willen" are mutually complementary (BPG, p. 3*). Criticism, as Pope had first explained, is "der Musen Aufwärterinn" (BPG, p. 13*)[44]. This was also the cornerstone of the Enlightenment as a whole.

The present study challenges the commonly-held view, even among recent interpretations, that the period 1720-1740 was a

time of strict neo-classicism ("strenger Aufklärungs-
klassizismus") and that it is not until 1740 that one may
speak of a new period of literary achievement (of a "Blüte-
zeit") in Germany.[45] We do not deny that, in their poetological works, Gottsched and Breitinger, in particular, drew
upon similar works from Greek and Roman antiquity and that, to
this extent, their endeavors may be termed classicistic. But
to dismiss their attempts to provide a practical guide for
artists (thereby encouraging the development of a distinctly
German literature) as essentially the poison for creative
productivity exaggerates and misrepresents the true intention
and actual content of their work. René Wellek's warning that
the term "rationalist" is misleading, "if it is interpreted to
mean that neo-classical criticism conceives of art as a con-
struct of the conscious intelligence to the exclusion of
feeling, imagination, and even the unconscious"[46], must be
born in mind, if the term is to have any validity at all.

Neither Gottsched's, nor Breitinger's critical poetics
(1730 and 1740, respectively) contains any denial that it is
the creative imagination which is the true source of art. The
fact that neither poetologist[47] dwells on the subject reveals,
not that they had failed to perceive of the creative imagination as the key to artistic achievement, but that this fact
was so self-evident that it needed comparatively little ela-
boration. What their critical poetics clarify is how feeling
and the creative imagination are to express themselves, in
order to assure the greatest effect. Any attempt to explain

the secrets of the creative process was assumed to be futile.
For the creative process was, and remains, a dark mystery. It
was termed a "gift". Nonetheless, the outward manifestations of
this creative energy could be known. Therefore, the question of
form became the proper object of a poetological work.[48]

It is important to remember that, no matter how fantastic
or allegedly unrestrained the creative imagination, for the
artist there is always the question of what form his work is to
take. This is the central difference between the artist and
the common man. For man's imaginings often ramble on, un-
checked and unrestrained, where, for the artist, there is
always the awareness that he must give form to imagination, if
he wishes to be truly successful. The artist's imagination is
not wild. It is creative. And creation implies form. The
allegation, then, that the poetological works of Opitz,
Gottsched and Breitinger (among others) restrict the "free
play" of the imagination is founded upon the erroneous assumption that the creative imagination is free to do as it chooses.
The thought that form restricts and thereby gives shape and
depth to the workings of the creative imagination is particularly evident in the poetics and aesthetics of the early
German Aufklärung.

Furthermore, the so-called "rules" contained within these
works are to be understood as general conclusions based on
what these theoreticians understood to be scientific observation, and not as the result of the self-satisfying indulgence
of supposedly omniscient law-givers. They conceived of their

critical poetics as practical guides for the artist and believed that they had discovered those principles which had
informed the greatest of literary works of art.

The early German Aufklärer were well aware that, if the
dream of a truly national literature was to become a reality,
the support of the public, of aristocracy and bourgeosie alike,
was imperative. It is for this reason that the early enlightened critics placed such a great emphasis upon the edifying effect
of which literature is capable. That such a dream shortly became reality is due to none other than the early German
Aufklärer.

Our critical reassessment investigates primarily three
aspects of the poetic and aesthetic theory of the early German
Aufklärung. The first chapter surveys the major writings
which have as their focus the imitation of nature. This is
followed by a study of poetic enthusiasm and creative imagination as perceived by the early Aufklärer. The final chapter
discusses the important concepts of beauty at the time and
introduces the ideas of the distasteful and the sublime. For
the sake of clarity and consistency, we discuss these works in
order of their chronology, although we vary from this procedure when parallels and contrasts can be drawn.

CHAPTER I

OF CRITICAL POETICS AND IMITATION

> Da nun die Poesie eine Nachahmung
> der Schöpfung und der Natur nicht
> nur in dem Würcklichen, sondern
> auch in dem Möglichen ist, so muss
> ihre Dichtung, die eine Art der
> Schöpfung ist, ihre Wahrschein-
> lichkeit entweder in der Ueber-
> einstimmung mit den gegenwärtiger
> Zeit eingeführten Gesetzen und dem
> Laufe der Natur gründen, oder in
> den Kräften der Natur, welche sie
> bey andern Absichten nach unsern
> Begriffen hätte ausüben können
> (Johann Jacob Breitinger).

I. Gottsched's Versuch einer Critischen Dichtkunst

A. The Question of Originality

Johann Christoph Gottsched's (1700-1766) Versuch einer
Critischen Dichtkunst vor die Deutschen[1] is not a rule book,
the dictates of which the literary artist was expected to
follow unfailingly. The work is a treatise of poetics which
contains a restatement, similar to, and yet surpassing
Nicolas Boileau-Despréaux's Art poétique (1674)[2], of what
poetologists, tragedians, and other critics of art had been
saying at least since Aristotle's Poetics. Gottsched
addresses himself to this in the introduction to his work,
while referring to the three years he had spent in the home
of Bernhard Mencke[3]:

> Hier lernte ich alle alte Scribenten, alle
> ausländische Poeten, alle Criticos, und ihre
> Gegner kennen...Was mir nun Aristoteles,
> Longin, Horaz, Scaliger, Boileau, Dacier,

> Bossu, Perrault, Fenelon, St. Evremont,
> Fontenelle, Callieres, Furetiere, Shafftsbury,
> Steele, imgleichen Corneille und Racine in
> den Vorreden zu ihren Tragödien und a.m. die
> mir itzo nicht einfallen vor ein Licht gegeben;
> das werden diejenigen sich leicht vorstellen,
> so nur etliche davon gelesen haben. Hierzu
> sind nachmahls noch des Castelvetro, Muralts
> und Voltaire Beurtheilungen alter und neuer
> Poeten, imgleichen des Hn. Bodmers hieher
> gehörige Schrifften, gekommen, welche mich immer
> mehr in den alten Ideen befestiget, und meinem
> Gemüthe eine neue Befriedigung gegeben haben
> (VCD, "Vorrede", p. *7).

Enjoying no less than four editions between 1730 and 1751, this treatise is perhaps the most representative work of the early German Aufklärung concerning literature.

In his monumental survey of eighteenth century German literature, Hermann Hettner makes the following assessment of Gottsched's Critische Dichtkunst: "Es ist der Standpunkt Boileau's, aber verflacht und vergröbert"[4]. And, as recent as 1956, Bruno Markwardt could maintain: "Ein Originalwerk war die kritische Dichtkunst gewiß nicht"[5]. Such statements have been most instrumental in perpetuating the misunderstanding which, for so long, has marred the actual import of Gottsched's poetological endeavors.

In two of the most important chapters of his critical poetics, "Von dem Charaktere eines Poeten" (I,2) and "Von den drei Gattungen der poetischen Nachahmung und insonderheit von der Fabel" (I,4), Gottsched quotes Boileau seven times. Six of these references are found in his chapter on the character of the poet. However, it is impossible to ignore the many quotations from such writers as Horace (also quoted seven

times), Rachel (4), Canitz (2), and Opitz (2), in addition
to the frequent references to Aristotle and Vergil. In a
third chapter, "Von dem Wunderbaren in der Poesie" (I,5),
quotations from various writers serve primarily as examples
which Gottsched believes will support his thesis. In "Von
Tragödien und Trauerspielen" (II,10), the critic does, in
fact, rely substantially upon Boileau's remarks. No less
authoritative, however, is Horace, who is quoted as often as
Boileau. As Aristotle and Horace are the main authorities who
Gottsched cites in his chapter on tragedy, so it is Horace and
Boileau upon whom he relies in his thesis concerning comedy.

However, to base our judgment simply on the frequency of
quotations and references is not sufficient. Hettner makes yet
another accusation. "Wo wissenschaftliche Begründung er-
forderlich war, erscheint immer nur eine Belegstelle aus
Boileau."[6]

Since Gottsched informs us that the brunt of his attempts
to formulate a critical poetics will concern the imitation of
nature, it is appropriate to consider the importance of quotation in his work by directing our attention to the chapter,
"Von den drei Gattungen der poetischen Nachahmung und insonderheit von der Fabel" (I,4).

In this chapter, only two of the five main quotations
serve as "scientific evidence", as Hettner understands it.
The first is by Boileau. The second is from Horace.

Following Gottsched's classification of description as
the lowest form of imitation, we encounter a quotation by

Boileau, where the French theoretician attacks Scuderi for overloading his descriptions of objects. With Boileau's assistance, Gottsched endeavors to support the thesis that the poet who is unable to make his descriptions concise and who tirelessly insists upon "painting" verbal pictures and images is actually an irksome writer who perpetuates loathsomeness among his readers. Throughout the remainder of the chapter, Boileau is not quoted again.

More interesting, in view of Gottsched's method of quotation, is his defense of Horace. Here, Gottsched demonstrates his originality and asserts that the common opinion that Horace had classified the genre of comedy under the category of base ("niedrige"), as opposed to elevated ("hohe") plots, is false. Gottsched then maintains that Horace was at times quite supportive of comedy because of its "pathetische, feurige und erhabene Sprache" (VCD, p. 128). Such a positive example of Gottsched's method of argumentation shows the critic in the act of defending, not a matter-of-fact, or moralistically mundane poetic style, but an emotionally-charged language which bears some resemblance to Bodmer's defense of an "erhabene Schreibart" some sixteen years later in the Critische Briefe (1746).

The last, fairly extensive portion of the chapter leads into Gottsched's often-quoted definition of the plot. It is obvious that this definition proceeds from Aristotle and Horace, even though it stands alone. Boileau is not mentioned.[7]

To maintain, therefore, that Gottsched's <u>Critische</u>
<u>Dichtkunst</u> is no more than a shallow and crude reformulation of
Boileau's standpoint is to ignore the influence which numerous
other writers had upon Gottsched.[8] Furthermore, the charge
that this work was not an original study overlooks Gottsched's
open admission of the same in the introduction. Nevertheless,
Gottsched's <u>Versuch einer Critischen Dichtkunst vor die</u>
<u>Deutschen</u> is the first comprehensive treatise on poetics of its
kind in the history of German literature. In this respect, it
may be viewed as an original contribution.

It was Gottsched's sincere hope that, if German artists
could master the principles which underly the great works of
art, in much the same way as Raphael had learned to emulate
Michelangelo, the dawn of a truly great and autonomous national
literature would be hastened.[9] It was Gottsched's <u>Critische</u>
<u>Dichtkunst</u>, as a compilation of the most essential insights in-
to the production of great literary works of art from ancient
to modern times, which, more than any single work of the German
<u>Aufklärung</u>, hastened the emergence of a national literature.
That this was a successful endeavor is attributable to
Gottsched's historical awareness that, in order for a national
literature to be fruitful, it needed to be grounded on a firm
foundation--the foundation of the past.

B. The Imitation Theory

From the title of Gottsched's critical poetics we learn
that "das innere Wesen der Poesie" consists "in einer Nach-

ahmung der Natur". Where for Aristotle, "artists imitate men
involved in action"[10], Gottsched expands on the Aristotelian
dictum and describes the poet as "ein geschickter Nachahmer
aller natürlichen Dinge" (VCD, p. 82).

In I,4 of the Critische Dichtkunst, "Von den drei
Gattungen der poetischen Nachahmung, und insonderheit von der
Fabel", Gottsched divides imitation into a number of levels
indicating a progression from the lowest to the highest, or
from the merely acceptable to the best forms of imitation

The lowest ("geringste") type of imitation for Gottsched
consists in "einer blossen Beschreibung", or, at best, "einer
sehr lebhaften Schilderey von einer natürlichen Sache" (VCD,
p. 118). The ability, then, to describe natural occurrences
constitutes the lowest type of imitation. Yet, even this type
of imitation is not without some life. The illustration can be
lively ("lebhaft"). Furthermore, Gottsched notes that these
descriptions have some affinity to painting. The object which
the poet contemplates is such, "die man...vor die Augen malet
und gleichsam mit lebendigen Farben entwirft...als ob sie
würcklich zugegen wäre" (VCD, p. 118). And yet, this type of
imitation, in Gottsched's estimation, far exceeds the kind of
imitation characteristic of painting. Comparing the art of
painting to the art of poetry, Gottsched maintains the following: "Diese [die Malerkunst] kan nur vor die Augen malen, der
Poet dagegen vor alle Sinne Schildereyen machen" (VCD, p. 119).
Carrying the thought even further, the critic exclaims, "Ja er

[der Poet] kan endlich auch geistliche Dinge, als da sind innerliche Bewegungen des Hertzens und die verborgensten Gedancken beschreiben und abmahlen" (VCD, p. 119). The poet, through careful study of nature, has the ability, then, to uncover the inner workings of the heart and to comprehend the most secret thoughts of man.

That type of imitation which, in Gottsched's understanding, demands much more skill occurs "wenn der Poet selbst die Person eines andern spielet" (VCD, p. 120). However, the poetic imitation of passions must be exact and the poet is expected to allow the characters of his art to speak as they might in the real world.

It is with this second type of imitation that the effect which the poet's art evokes becomes a criterion of judgment for the literary critic. And it is precisely on this point that Hofmannswaldau's Heldenbriefe are said to fail.[11] Much neglected, particularly in this respect, are Gottsched's explanatory notes to his translation of Horace's Ars poetica which prefaces the Versuch einer Critischen Dichtkunst.[12] It is here that the influence of the rhetorical tradition upon Gottsched is most conspicuous.[13] For Gottsched, poetry must move the beholder, if it is to be successful. More than beautiful words are required of the poet.

> Schöne Worte machens noch nicht aus, dass
> ein Gedichte schön ist: es muss auch durch
> den Inhalt einnehmen, bewegen, entzücken,
> ja fast gar bezaubern. Alle poetische
> Blümchen, aller Zibeth, Mosch und Ambra,
> Nectar und Ambrosia ist vergeblich:...wenn

> die innerliche Beschaffenheit der Gedancken
> nicht das Hertz führet, die Affecte[14] rege
> macht, und das Gemüthe des Lesers oder
> Zuschauers in Schauspielen nach Gefallen
> hin und her treibet (<u>VCD</u>, p. 18).[15]

In revering the free invention of plot over all other
types of imitation, Gottsched generalized Aristotle's statement that the soul of tragedy is the plot (Poetics, 1450[a]).
Plot now constitutes the soul of the art of poetry in general:
"Die Fabel ist hauptsächlich das jenige, so die Seele der
gantzen Dicht-Kunst ist..." (<u>VCD</u>, p. 123).[16]

For Gottsched, every plot must contain something true, as
well as something false.

> In der That muss eine jede Fabel was Wahres
> und was Falsches in sich haben, nämlich einen
> moralischen Lehrsatz; der gewiss wahr sein muss,
> und eine Einkleidung desselben in eine gewisse
> Begebenheit, die sich aber niemahls zugetragen
> hat und also falsch ist (<u>VCD</u>, p. 124).

There is no question that Gottsched views poetry as being
morally purposive. But the more interesting question is how
this is to be achieved.

Of particular interest here is the demand for creativity
in the invention of plot which Gottsched designates as "das
Falsche". "Das Falsche" is an imaginative occurrence--an
occurrence which has never taken place in the real world, but
which serves to heighten interest among the beholders of art.[17]
What is significant, however, is the call for a certain veiling
("Einkleidung") of the moral content of a work of art. What
this means is that, in the course of events, whatever moral
instruction does occur it will necessarily be <u>indirect</u>. For

direct moralizing causes displeasure.

> Die gründlichste Sittenlehre ist vor den
> grossen Haufen der Menschen viel zu mager
> und trocken. Denn die Schärfe in Vernunft-
> schlüssen ist nicht vor den gemeinen
> Verstand unstudirter Leute (VCD, p. 139).

But not only must the moral lesson be indirect. It must also be limited in length in order to be pleasing:

> Die Sittenlehren in Theatralischen Poesien
> müssen kürtzlich gefasset seyn, und nicht
> über ein paar Zeilen austragen (="erbaulich
> schreiben") (VCD, p. 41).

It is this express call for the limited and indirect conveyance of the moral content of a work of art which frees Gottsched from the allegation of didacticism which for so long has distorted Gottsched's true message.[18]

In the course of his treatise, Gottsched has become more sensitive toward the wishes of the general public. If they consider the most thorough and basic moral to be too sterile and uninteresting, then it is the poet who must make amends. Afterall, "die nackte Wahrheit" pleases only "philosophische Köpfe" (VCD, p. 139). Poetry is not philosophy.[19] With this realization, Gottsched proceeds to support the Horacean dictum that poetry must delight, as well as instruct. "Die Poesie... lehret und belustiget und schicket sich vor Gelehrte und Ungelehrte" (VCD, p. 139).

Gottsched's call for the hidden moral import of poetry and the free invention of plot reveal more of the actual nature of his theory of imitation.

> Ich glaube derowegen eine Fabel am besten
> zu beschreiben, wenn ich sage, sie sei eine
> unter gewissen Umständen mögliche, aber nicht

> würcklich vorgefallene Begebenheit, darunter
> eine nützliche moralische Wahrheit verborgen
> liegt (VCD, p. 125). [emphasis mine].

It has become increasing clear that the main accent of

Gottsched's pronouncements concerning the imitation of nature

is upon the creation of possible occurrences which are in

harmony with the law of probability. In referring to imita-

tion in dramatic art ("theatralische Poesie"), the critic

maintains the following:

> ...hier muss ein Poet alles, was von dem
> auftretenden Helden oder was es sonst ist,
> würcklich und der Natur gemäss hätte
> geschehen können, so genau nachahmen, dass
> man nichts unwahrscheinliches dabey
> wahrnehmen könne (VCD, p. 122).

For Martin Opitz, as well, the emphasis lies upon the creative

imitation of nature:

> ...und soll man auch wissen, das die
> gantze Poeterey im nachäffen der Natur
> bestehe, und die dinge nicht so sehr
> beschreibe wie sie sein, als wie sie
> etwan sein köndten oder solten.[20]

As late as 1760, poetic imitation, for Gottsched, meant

the imitation of beautiful nature, by which he understood

"nicht das Wahre, welches wirklich ist, sondern das Wahre,

das seyn kann, mit allen Vollkommenheiten, die sich zusammen

schicken".[21] Although the artist must imitate nature, this

imitation must never be slavish ("knechtisch"). It must be

creative, as well as verisimilar.

> Jedoch muss diese Nachahmung nicht knechtisch
> seyn; sondern der Künstler muss theils eine
> gute Wahl treffen; und theils das Gewählte
> in aller Vollkommenheit darstellen. Man saget
> daher, man müsse der schönen Natur nachahmen:
> ...Soll die Nachahmung selbst so vollkommen
> seyn, als es möglich ist, so muss sie diese

> zwo Eigenschaften haben: die Richtigkeit und
> die Freyheit. Jene regieret nämlich die
> Nachahmung; diese belebet sie. Weil es aber
> schwer ist, beyde zu verbinden: so fehlen
> viele Künstler.[22] [italics mine].

Accurate description and creative freedom are therefore
essential to Gottsched's theory of imitation. For where the
former assures authenticity, the latter enlivens the artistic
representation.

Gottsched's theory of imitation has been misrepresented.
A. Köster (1925) assails Gottsched for his alleged perpetua-
tion of "sklavische Nachahmung"[23], while H. Wolff believes
that Gottsched's theory constitutes merely "ein schroffer
Realismus".[24] R. Newald (1951), whose work is representative
of traditional attitudes with respect to the history of
German literature, chastises Gottsched for his lack of creativity.[25] And J. Birke (1966), by holding Gottsched accountable
to Christian Wolff, is not able to perceive of Gottsched's
formulations as in any way transcending naturalism.[26]

Susi Bing (1934), however, stresses that to speak of
naturalism in Gottsched's case is to distort his theory of
imitation.[27] W. Bender (1966), in referring to Bing's work,
comments further on the basic commonality between Gottsched
and Breitinger on the question of the imitation of nature.[28]
And W. Rieck (1972), in taking issue with Birke, points out
Gottsched's allowances for creative expression.[29]

As we have demonstrated, the essence of art, for
Gottsched, consists in the delicate balance between verisimilitude and creativity in the imitation of nature. Even the

lowest type of imitation, for Gottsched, that of mere description, is capable of producing "eine sehr lebhafte
Schilderey". Accurate reflection and creative freedom, the
plausible and the probable, combine to create a truly natural
and lively poetry. In this way, the creative power of the
artist gained ever greater freedom.

II. Breitinger's Critische Dichtkunst

A. The Question of Influence

It is quite clear that Johann Jacob Breitinger (1701-
1776), in formulating his critical poetics[30], drew extensively
upon the work of Aristotle, Horace, Leibniz, Addison, Dubos and
Muratori, to name some of the most influential. For the key
concepts of his poetics--the imitation theory, which Batteux,
in 1746, was to redefine as the one principle common to all
the arts[31], and the idea of the arousal of pleasure among the
beholders of art--Breitinger was indebted to Aristotle[32].
Horace's maxim, aut prodesse volunt, aut delectare poetae[33],
the thought that art must please, as well as instruct, re-
tained its hold over Breitinger, although, as we shall see, the
critic favors the moving of the public above all else. Whenever Breitinger speaks of the usefulness of art, he means the
furtherance of the ideal of human perfectibility, an idea which
stems from Leibniz.[34] Breitinger's concepts of "das Neue" and
"das Wunderbare", the latter of which informed Jean Paul's
idea of the same[35], came upon Breitinger by way of Addison's
formulations concerning the new and the marvelous[36]. Dubos'
thoughts on the similarity between painting and poetry and the

arousal of pleasure informed the theoretician's poetics[37]. And for his distinction between historical and poetic truth and the choice of the proper means of imitation, Breitinger makes reference to Muratori[38]. Yet, far from being a collage of collected thoughts, Breitinger's Critische Dichtkunst is a powerful Wirkungspoetik, which, in the critical analysis of what he understood to be the best ancient and modern works of art and poetological treatises, defined better than any work in German before it the creativity of the poetic spirit.

Only recently have Klaus Dockhorn's insights into the impact of the rhetorical tradition upon the development of poetics begun to have an effect on interpretation[39]. Even the most superficial acquaintance with the Critische Dicht-kunst will reveal the enormous effect which Aristotle's Rhetoric, Cicero's De Oratore and Quintilian's Institutionis oratoriae had upon Breitinger's poetic theory. Although B. Markwardt is correct in referring to Breitinger's poetology as a Wirkungspoetik[40], he fails to show that the source of the critic's concern for moving the reader is to be found in the art of rhetoric[41]. That this tradition also had a profound influence on Bodmer as well is evidenced by his Critische Abhandlung von dem Wunderbaren in der Poesie, where the critic equates "das Siegel einer durchdringenden Gewalt auf die Gemüther", which characterizes Milton's Paradise Lost, with the "Siegel einer durchdringenden Beredtsamkeit"[42].

It is a curious fact that Breitinger is infatuated with the power of the artist to move the audience. The critic

focuses primarily upon the artist's ability to tap "die
Kräfte der Natur" (CD, I, pp. 54, 136, 272) and to generate
through his art an overwhelming and lasting effect on the
reader. This is confirmed by his repeated references to the
"Kraft der poetischen Mahlerey" (CD, I, p. 30), and the "Kraft
der Poesie" (CD, I, p. 133); to the "unendliche Kraft des
Schöpfers der Natur" (CD, I, p. 135) with respect to the
"Macht des Poeten" and the "Kraft seiner Einbildung" (CD, I,
273), as well as with the "Kraft und Würckung der Vorstellung"
(CD, I, p. 84). It is with this "bezaubernde Kraft der Dicht-
Kunst" (CD, I, p. 141), with poesy as "eine Kunst-volle
Zauberin" (CD, I, p. 33, where he acknowledges his debt to the
rhetoricians) that Breitinger is most concerned. In this light,
Breitinger's critical poetics becomes a testimonial to the power
which the poet possesses to move his reader.

It is this concern for the irrational which reveals the
profound influence of the rhetorical tradition upon Breitinger's
poetics[43]. It is the artistic vacillation of _ethos_ and _pathos_
(Aristotle), or _conciliare_ and _movere_ (Cicero, Quintilian),
that is, of the development of character through softness of
speech and powerful emotion, which lies at the heart of the art
of _persuasio_, and which informs the poetic, aesthetic and
dramatic theory of the 18th Century. Indeed, it has been
suggested that the complementary pairs, "anmutend-gross",
"schön-erhaben", "Anmut-Würde", which characterize the aesthetic
theory of 18th Century Germany, find their origin in the basic
pair of _ethos_ and _pathos_[44].

Nevertheless, it is important to note Breitinger's contribution to the development of poetics as an independent
field of endeavor vis a vis the art of rhetoric. Though
Breitinger never denies the influence of rhetoric upon his
thought, in the final analysis, he considers the poet superior
to the orator, and the art of poetry more demanding than the
art of persuasion:

> ...weil die Einbildung der Poeten
> heftiger soll und muss erreget werden,
> als der Redner, so kan desswegen der
> Poet künstlichere, fremdere und
> ungewöhnlichere Bilder, als die
> einfältigen sind, formieren, damit er
> mittelst derselben nach Belieben
> diesen oder jenen Affect in das
> Gemüthe der Leser oder Hörer mit
> Gewalt hineindrücke (CD, I, p. 337).

Again, when Breitinger speaks of the indispensability of in-
fusing speech with imaginative turns of speech ("Einbildungen")
he distinguishes between the orator's and the poet's use of the
same and concludes that both uses are required, if the poet is
to truly move the heart of the reader.

> Diese [die Redner] brauchen sie
> [die Einbildungen] , das Gemüthe in
> Bestürzung zu setzen, jene [die
> Poeten] die Sachen deutlich zu
> schildern: Beyden müssen sie dienen,
> das Hertz zu rühren (CD, I, p. 323).

This deepseated concern for moving the beholder is central
both to Breitinger's and to Bodmer's poetic theories and is
rooted in their assumptions concerning the nature of man. Most
inconsistent with the alleged dominance of rationalism at the
time of the Aufklärung is Breitinger's insistence "dass auch
die meisten Menschen mehr nach einem sinnlichen Ergetzen

streben, und mehr durch das Gefühl als durch den Verstand geleitet werden... (CD, I, p. 80). What is natural and pleasant to man is "die Unruh und Bewegung der Gemüthes-Leidenschaften" (CD, I, p. 85). And, with respect to the reading public, Breitinger maintains "dass die Leute allezeit lieber die Bücher lesen werden, die sie rühren, als die, so sie unterrichten" (CD, I, p. 86). Or, as Bodmer was to note in the Neue Critische Briefe of 1749:

> Sie wollen Empfindungen, sie wollen Neigungen haben. Die Schriften, die sie erleuchten, gebähren bald Verdruss bey ihnen, wenn sie nicht daneben das Herz rühren. Und da der Uberdruss ihnen allezeit eine grössere Last ist, als die Unwissenheit, so legen sie ein Buch bald aus den Händen, welches sie nur unterrichtet, und nehmen dafür ein anders, das sie rühret[45]. [italics mine].

As is evident from the aforementioned, Breitinger's poetology favors the moving more than the instruction of the beholder of art.

B. The Imitation of Nature

Before entering into a discussion of Breitinger's theory of imitation, it is necessary to first clarify his concepts of reality and nature.

For Breitinger, reality, in the broadest sense of the term, embraces the sum total of creation, and includes both the visible and invisible worlds. The visible world is the materially real world and contains everything "was der Prüf-fung der Sinnen unterworffen ist" (CD, I, p. 55). The invisible world is the world of Milton's Paradise Lost and Klopstock's Der Messias, the domain of angels and higher spirits. This world, which lies within and beyond external reality, is, in Breitinger's estimation, as real, i.e. possible, as the visible world, "da sie den Grund und die Quelle aller Würcklichkeit in sich hat" (CD, I, p. 56). The truth of all things belonging to the invisible world is grounded "in dem Zeugniss der Sinnen... dem Zeugniss des Gewissens, und der göttlichen Offenbarung" (CD, I, p. 55), i.e. the possibility of their existence[46], free of contradiction and regulated by the omnipotence of the creator of nature which is God. The theological, mystical and metaphysical base of Breitinger's concept of reality informs his entire poetic theory.

Nature, "oder vielmehr der Schöpfer, der in derselben und durch dieselbe würcket" (CD, I, p. 54), is, for Breitinger, what it had been for Leibniz and Aristotle: potentiality, energy or "Kraft", which, as in the entelechy, strives toward a higher realisation and perfection, i.e. a higher goal. Nature is dynamic, containing within it inexhaustible potentiality which gives rise to unlimited possibility. Drawing upon Leibniz, "der grosse Weltweise unseres Deutschlands", and Baumgarten[47], Breitinger understood that the imitation of this the best of all possible worlds (CD, I, p. 268) actually meant the imitation of the ideal. For in this world the greatest variety imaginable was united with the greatest possible order. Nature was "vollkommen und unverbesserlich" (CD, I, p. 271)-- "ein unerschöpflicher Brunnen des Neuen, worinnen man beständig zu schöpfen findet" (CD, I, pp. 106, 113-114).

The rather prevalent thought of the time, then, that art

could improve upon the apparent imperfections of nature was, for Breitinger, fallacious. The artistic act to which the proponents of this idea were referring was in actuality nothing more and nothing less than the transformation of the real into the possible (CD, I, p. 268). The artist does not create new originals ("Urwercke"), but actually imitates nature in its possible manifestations.

The clearest definition of poesy is found in the sixth chapter of the Critische Dichtkunst, entitled "Von dem Wunderbaren und dem Wahrscheinlichen". Here, poesy is defined as a "Nachahmung der Schöpfung und der Natur...in dem Würcklichen...und in dem Möglichen" (CD, I, p. 136).

For Breitinger, poetic imitation embraces both the imitation of nature as it exists in the actual world which surrounds us, and as it could possibly exist, if nature had so intended.

The inferior of poetic imitations, the one requiring the least artistic acumen, is the mere imitation of the actual manifestations of nature. The one who imitates these originals ("Originale"="Urbilder") is a mere copier ("Abdrücker", CD, I, p. 55).

The true artist, while at times drawing upon actual historical events or other natural phenomena for his material, will embrace that "allesvermögende Kraft des Schöpfers der Natur" (CD, I, p. 56). It is therefore incumbent upon the artist to imitate nature, not simply in its actuality, but in accordance with its creative potentiality. And it is on this point that the true import and strength of Breitinger's poetics is felt. For by tapping the creative energy of Nature the poet's art is capable of extending itself as far as ("eben so weit") the forces of nature. The "Grund-Regel" for the poet, as well as the painter, is "dass sie in ihrer Nachahmung alleine auf die Kräfte der Natur sehen" (CD, I, p. 63). By looking within nature, by studying its laws, that which lies hidden ("verborgen") in nature, and its resultant manifestations, the poet comes to a recognition of what is possible. Through this study of the inner workings of nature and the resultant imitation of nature in its possible existence ("die Nachahmung der Natur in dem Möglichen"), the poet is engaged in what Breitinger perceives to be "das eigene und Haupt-Werck der Poesie" (CD, I, p. 57).

It is the creative imitation of nature which receives the greatest emphasis here.

> Denn ich darf vor gewiss setzen, dass die
> Dicht-Kunst, insoferne sie von der Historie
> unterschieden ist, ihre Originale und die
> Materie ihrer Nachahmung nicht so fast aus
> der gegenwärtigen, als vielmehr aus der Welt
> der möglichen Dinge entlehnen müsse (CD, I, p. 57).

In this significant distinction between mere and creative imitation, there is commonality between Breitinger and Johann Sulzer (1720-1779). Although Sulzer, in his Theorie der schönen Künste (1771-1774), distinguishes between three kinds of imitation, the last two divisions are equivalent to Breitinger's characterization of the "Abdrücker" and the creative imitator.

The first type of imitation for Sulzer is mere "Nachäffung":

"So machen viel seichte Köpfe aus den schönen Künsten ein
Kinderspiel, und äffen die Werke derselben nach, wie etwa
Kinder Soldaten spielen"[48]. The second kind of imitation is
"die knechtische und ängstliche" (TKW, III, p. 487), which
Gottsched had opposed as well, (see p. 9). Such "Nachahmer"
(TKW, III, p. 486) are said to have actually reflected upon the
originals of nature, but imitate a great deal which is in-
essential to their purpose, and therefore produce a work which
contains "viel unschikliches, oder gar ungereimtes" (TKW, III,
p. 487). "Also kann diese Art der Nachahmung ein im Grunde
sonst gutes und schikliches Werk verderben und lächerlich
machen" (TKW, III, p. 487). That type of imitation which
characterizes the work of the genuine artist is "die freye und
verständige" (TKW, III, p. 487). In taking the originals of
nature as his point of departure, the genuine "Nachfolger"
(TKW, III, p. 489) of nature shapes these originals in accordance with his own intentions and, by this means, creates "ein
wahres Originalwerk" (TKW, III, p. 487). True imitation is
therefore creative, not menial.

Such imitation for Breitinger, however, must be achieved
in accordance with the law of probability. In keeping with his
distinction between historical and poetic truth, Breitinger
maintains that the poet can attain his objectives "bloss durch
die Wahrscheinlichkeit", without concern for historical truth
(CD, I, pp. 58-59). The probable is grounded in the "würcklich
eingeführte Gesetze und der gegenwärtige Laufe der Natur" (CD,

I, p. 59) and is, for the majority of people, "eben so wahr, als das so würcklich geschehen ist" (CD, I, p. 59).

Like Gottsched before him and Sulzer after him (TKW, III, p. 487), Breitinger adheres to the theory of correspondence. The more perfect work of art will reflect a correspondence between the representations ("Abbilder") of art and their originals in nature: "Je grösser und offenbarer die Aehnlichkeit mit dem Urbild ist, desto mehr Licht und Wahrheit hat das Gemählde" (CD, I, p. 67). Although this has been pointed out, and the commonality between Breitinger and Gottsched on this point has been noted,[49] the actual reasons for this insistence upon verisimilitude in art have either been overlooked or simply dismissed as seemingly insignificant. In Breitinger's poetics, however, there is an unmistakable and overriding concern for the effect which art has upon the reader. And it is precisely in imitating nature creatively that Breitinger believes the reader can be moved and most powerfully affected. For "das poetische Wahre, welches der Grundstein alles Ergetzens ist,...sey eine deu t liche Uebereinstimmung des ähnlichen Gemähldes mit solchen Urbildern, die in dem Reiche der Natur anzutreffen, und also möglich sind" (CD, I, p. 67). The specific problem which Breitinger raises in his chapter on imitation (I,3) concerns the emulation through art of the effect which the forces of nature are capable of having upon man. The problem of poetic art, then, is understood as the creation of an effect upon the reader which is as lasting as that of nature. And it is precisely through the illusion or semblance of truth which is attained in the imitation of nature that art can achieve this effect.

> Auf dieser Aehnlichkeit und Uebereinstimmung
> der Nachahmung der Natur beruhet nun einestheils
> die lebhafte Deutlichkeit der Schildereyen, von
> welcher die wunderbare Kraft die Phantasie zu
> rühren entstehet, die uns nöthigt, bey Anschauung
> einer Schilderey bey uns selbst zu sagen: In
> Wahrheit ist es eben das, was ich gesehen, was ich
> gehöret habe; oder was ich mit meinen Augen sehen,
> mit meinen Ohren horen würde, wenn mir das
> Original von dieser Sache vor Augen oder zu Ohren
> käme (CD, I, p. 66).

It is by way of this "geschickte Nachahmung" (CD, I, p. 70f.) that the poet's art is able to have a lasting impression upon the reader.

But why imitation? Not only does Breitinger agree with Aristotle's insight that imitation is natural to man and that it is pleasing in and of itself (CD, I, p. 68), but he refers specifically to the second chapter of Aristotle's Rhetoric while noting the twofold source of enjoyment (CD, I, p. 71). The subject matter ("Materie") of imitation is said to cause enjoyment because of the expansion of our knowledge which results from perceiving certain truths of nature. The amazement ("Verwunderung") which we experience in beholding a work of art is understood as the result of the art of imitation ("die Kunst der Nachahmung") itself. So that it is both the object and the manner of imitation which accounts for the pleasure we receive from a work of art. And it is the art of imitation which, even more than nature itself, has the power to captivate the

attention of the beholder and render him spellbound! "Die
Nachahmung hat in der That mehr Kraft, die Aufmercksamkeit der
Leute zu unterstützen, als die Natur selbst" (CD, I, p. 72).
For "die Copie ziehet uns stärcker an sich, als das Original"
(CD, I, p. 72).

Breitinger's argument here is based on the assumption
that man's curiosity is generally insatiable and that he derives
unending pleasure from comparing. The emphasis, then, is upon
man's capacity to discern the similarities and differences
among things, that is, upon what was then understood as Witz[50].
And this is said to be particularly effective if the object of
imitation is already familiar to the beholder, as, for example,
in painting.

> Stellet uns die Nachahmung einen bekannten
> Gegenstand vor Augen, wovon wir allbereit
> einen Abdruck im Kopf haben, so nöthigt sie
> uns zugleich die Nachahmung mit dem Urbild,
> die Kräfte der Kunst mit den Kräften der
> Natur, die Empfindungen, welche die Kunst
> hervorbringet, mit denen Begriffen und
> Empfindungen, so die würcklichen Gegenstände
> selbst in unserm Gemüthe hinterlassen haben,
> zu vergleichen, und von ihrer Uebereinstimmung
> und Aehnlichkeit zu urtheilen...(CD, I, p. 72).

It is particularly in this "Gemüthes-Beschäftigung" whereby
the copy is compared with the original, i.e. judged, that man
comes to a profound awareness of and appreciation for his own
capabilities (CD, I, p. 73). By presenting to the beholder
familiar representations, the artist raises man to the position
of judge ("Richter", CD, I, p. 73). So it is by appealing to
man's self-esteem ("Eigenliebe")[51] that the poet pleasantly

flatters the beholder and thereby engages him in the learning
process (CD, I, p. 73).

And what occurs when the originals are not familiar to the
onlooker? Comparison still goes on, "da wir nemlich diese
unbekannten Bilder mit andern ähnlichen und bekannten vergleich-
en, und aus Zusammenhaltung der Umstände entscheiden, ob sie
möglich und wahrscheinlich seyen" (CD, I, pp. 74-75), but
amazement now over the ability of the artist to create and
overwhelm us "mit prächtigen Einbildungen von unsrer Würde"
(CD, I, p. 75) overcomes us.

Besides setting our soul into motion, i.e. satisfying both
our intellectual and emotional natures, art has the special
power to purify our emotions (esp. that of fear, CD, I, p. 76).
Yet we are spared any repugnant or adverse effect from the objects which are presented before us because art is but an imitation of nature. Art, then, in Breitinger's estimation, is
essentially play, in the Schillerian sense, which produces "ein
reines Ergetzen" (CD, I, p. 75).

Breitinger's thoughts on imitation do reflect considerable
agreement with Aristotle's thoughts on the same. But where
Aristotle remains content in his definition of a poet (as well
as a painter) as a "maker of likenesses" (Poetics, 1460[b]),
Breitinger shows some commonality with the essentially mystical
interpretation of imitation, as found, for example, in Scaliger's
Poetics[52]. By insisting that the poet must tap the powers of
nature and fervently study the inner workings of nature,

Breitinger's call for the imitation of nature touches upon
the idea of the poet as an imitator of the art of God.
Ultimately, perfection was the goal of art, and perfection
suggests piety. In this, the best of all possible worlds,
the artist was to seek out and give shape to the ideal order
which underlies nature. The artist, then, is a discoverer of
concealed nature (beauty), i.e. a "Nachfolger" of creation,
whose peculiar power, for Breitinger, lies in his ability to
shape and educate man.

The creative freedom which Gottsched allowed in the artistic
imitation of nature now becomes the very center of Breitinger's
poetology. But whereas Gottsched had maintained a delicate
balance between plausibility and probability, Breitinger
emphasizes time and again the power of the artist to create new
possible worlds never before beheld by the human mind.

The poet is no longer perceived as "ein geschickter Nachahmer aller natürlichen Dinge", but rather as an imitator of the
art of God.

III. Johann Elias Schlegel on Imitation

Thus far, we have seen that it is the law of correspondence which unites Gottsched and Breitinger in their
investigations concerning the imitation of nature, as well as
the call for creative imitation. Verisimilitude in the complete
agreement between the artistic representation and its original
in nature was required of any genuine work of art for these
early Aufklärer. Nonetheless, an important question remains

unanswered in the poetology of Gottsched and Breitinger.
Since it is true that neither Gottsched·nor Breitinger ever
denied that the law of probability as it applies to art is
based, not upon the understanding ("Verstand"), but upon the
imagination ("Einbildung") of the beholder, the question of the
actual similarity of the artistic representation to the natural
phenomenon of which it claims to be a successful imitation remains open. For what is true to the imagination may often vary
from the truth of the object itself. The first Aufklärer to
critically investigate the law of correspondence in the imitation of nature was Johann Elias Schlegel (1718-1749).

> A.   Abhandlung, dass die Nachahmung der
>   Sache, der man nachahmet, zuweilen
>   unähnlich werden müsse (1741)[53]

As we have suggested, neither Gottsched nor Breitinger
seems to have been aware of the apparent discrepancy between the
call for creative imitation and the insistence upon the law of
correspondence. For the perceptions of the audience themselves
do not necessarily correspond to the true and actual nature of
things. This is Schlegel's point of departure. Indeed, his
entire argument rests on the assumption (of empiricists) that
the perceptions which man has of reality may at times conflict
with the true nature ("Beschaffenheit") of objects, and that
these deceptive ("falsch") conceptions are carried over to the
aesthetic experience. Thus, the artist, while imitating
nature, must be sensitive toward this fact, and, when necessary,
bring his representation into harmony, not with the actual

object, but with the idea ("Begriff") which the beholder of art possesses of the object under consideration.

> Ist es aber wahr, dass wir nachahmen, damit andre die Aehnlichkeit unsrer Bilder mit ihren Vorbildern bemerken, so müssen wir so nachahmen, dass unser Bild mit dem Begriffe, welchen andre von dem Vorbilde haben, übereinkommt. Denn nach ihren Begriffen werden sie uns richten...(ANS, p. 99).

It is with this "cabinet" (ANS, p. 100) of appearances, that the true artist will be concerned. Although the beholder, while perceiving a work of art, is actively engaged in making comparisons, the understanding is not used in the same way as if one were trying to discern the true nature of some physical relationship. For the comparison being made is that between the idea which one possesses and the artistic representation of some natural object. So that even in the act of comparing, the beholder is engaging his imagination. For Schlegel, this is the true nature of the aesthetic experience. Indeed, "auch so gar da, wo wir mit dem Verstande zur Wahrheit durchgedrungen sind, wird unsre Einbildungskraft unserm Verstande noch wiedersprechen" (ANS, p. 101). The ingeniousness of Schlegel's argument lies precisely in this distinction.

> Wir werden anders urtheilen, wenn wir die wahre Beschaffenheit der Sache untersuchen, und anders, wenn wir Vorbild und Bild in unsern Gedanken gegen einander halten (ANS, p. 101).

From this presupposition, Schlegel can thus conclude:

> Wenn also unsere Begriffe öfters falsch sind, und wenn wir dennoch die Bilder, die wir durch die Nachahmung hervorbringen, den Begriffen der Menschen ähnlich machen müssen: So folgt nothwendig, dass diese Bilder der Sache, der wir nachahmen, nicht nur zuweilen, sondern so

> oft unähnlich seyn müssen, als die Begriffe,
> nach denen die Menschen unsre Bilder
> beurtheilen werden, den Sachen selbst unähnlich
> sind (ANS, p. 101).

To be sure, Schlegel realizes the impossibility of total

adaptability to the concepts of the beholder. His main con-

cern, however, is that the audience be given full consideration

by the artist, in order to maximize the total effect of a work

of art.

In answer to the question why the artist should be con-

cerned with what others think, Schlegel explains that it is

because the artist wishes to arouse pleasure (ANS, p. 101).

The art of imitation, then, is judged in accordance with the

amount of pleasure it can generate: "Je mehr Vergnügen unsre

Nachahmung erweckt, desto schöner ist sie" (ANS, p. 101).

Dissimilarity, then, when furthering the cause of pleasure, is

allowed, if these conditions prevail (ANS, p. 101).

Although Schlegel expressly states that the experience of

correspondence does in fact arouse pleasure, he maintains that

such pleasure cannot be as powerful and lively in all things

(ANS, p. 102). For instance, he maintains that repulsive or

disgusting objects or occurrences will cause displeasure. At

the same time, however, such events are proper objects of

imitation. How, then, are such things to be presented artisti-

cally, without arousing displeasure? The answer lies in

Schlegel's rule of dissimilarity. For by varying somewhat in

the imitation of such an occurrence, the artist can avoid dis-

pleasure. The portrayal of death upon the stage, for instance,

should correspond to the kind of death the spectator would wish

upon himself and not to the imitation of the gruesomeness of
some actual death (ANS, p. 103). Therein lies the value of
dissimilar representation for Schlegel.

It is at this point that Schlegel presents a rather
amusing example. How, he asks, can one possibly imitate the
American Indians ("Amerikaner"), when our social mores forbid
the presentation of nakedness upon the stage. The answer lies
in clothing them, that is, varying from actuality.

Schlegel's "rule" of dissimilarity, then, allows for
basically four deviations from the law of correspondence.

> Ich habe dargethan, dass es recht sey,
> unähnlich zu seyn, wenn die Begriffe
> der Menschen von der Wahrheit abweichen:
> dass es nützlich sey, wenn das Vergnügen
> dadurch befordert wird; dass es eine
> Schuldigkeit sey, wenn man den Menschen
> dadurch Vorstellungen voll Eckel und
> Abscheu aus den Augen entziehet, oder
> wenn der Wohlstand einer vollkommenen
> Aehnlichkeit zuwieder ist (ANS, p. 104).

In concluding his essay, Schlegel adopts a polemical
attitude with respect to his new rule of dissimilarity.
"Aber", he reflects, "habe ich dadurch auch vielleicht der
Unähnlichkeit zu einer zügellosen Herrschaft verholfen? Habe
ich dadurch vielleicht ein Feld geöffnet, wo man ohne Regel
herumirren, und seine Hirngespinste für Nachahmungen verkaufen
wird?" "Nichts weniger, als dieses", he replies (ANS, p. 104)!
Despite such enthusiastic outbursts, however, Schlegel insists
that the artist must be careful to retain the semblance of
correspondence, that is, that he must conceal ("verbergen")
these instances with the appearance of consistency. "Denn es
macht allezeit Missvergnügen, wenn man die Unähnlichkeit

bemerket" (<u>ANS</u>, p. 105).

> Kurz, es ist kein Verbrechen, die Aehnlichkeit
> zu übertreten; aber es ist schon ein Fehler,
> sich merken zu lassen, dass man sie übertreten
> hat, und seine Unähnlichkeit den Sinnen seiner
> Richter empfindlich zu machen (<u>ANS</u>, p. 105).

Like Gottsched and Breitinger, Schlegel demands of the

poet a believable, i.e. plausible imitation. But what Gottsched

and Breitinger had failed to clarify was the fact that some

variance from nature was indeed essential to a successful work

of art. Allowance for <u>consistent</u> <u>inconsistency</u> in the creative

imitation of nature was first upheld by Johann Elias Schlegel.

B. <u>Abhandlung</u> <u>von</u> <u>der</u> <u>Nachahmung</u> (1742)[54]

Schlegel's <u>Abhandlung</u> <u>von</u> <u>der</u> <u>Nachahmung</u> is perhaps the

most in-depth study of the nature of poetic imitation among the

early <u>Aufklärer</u>. Whereas in his earlier essay on imitation,

he had cited those instances in which the artistic representa-

tion was allowed to vary from the original, Schlegel now sought

to clarify his position concerning the law of correspondence and

his rule of dissimilarity.

1. "Von der Nachahmung überhaupt"

The first part of his essay is an investigation into the

meaning of similarity ("Aehnlichkeit") in the artistic realm

and how it constitutes the essence of poetic imitation.

According to Schlegel, poetic imitation is said to exist

only when the poet has as his intention ("Absicht") the pro-

duction of something similar to an original ("Vorbild"). In-

deed, the imitation itself "muss bloss nach der Absicht beur-

theilet werden" (<u>AN</u>, 11, p. 123). And only in as much as
one realizes that this similarity which the poet produces is
not an end in itself, but a means to an end, will one be able to
judge the appearances which art transmits (<u>AN</u>, 11, p. 123).
When Schlegel considers the highest degree of correspondence
imaginable between the imitation and its original, he is led to
the conclusion that perfect correspondence is impossible. For
two things cannot be truly equivalent in every respect (<u>AN</u>,
12, p. 124). It therefore follows, "dass der höchste Grad der
Nachahmung [being a perfect agreement of the imitation with
every aspect of the original] von dem höchsten Grad der
Aehnlichkeit unterschieden sey" (<u>AN</u>, 12, p. 124).

It is therefore imperative that one remain cognisant of
Schlegel's insistence that an exact copy of an original is
unattainable--a point which critics have failed to note. Although he draws upon the Latin, <u>relatio</u>, and upon Christian
Wolff's understanding of what constitutes <u>Aehnlichkeit</u> (<u>AN</u>,
p. 116), Schlegel's main point is "dass diese Aehnlichkeit auch
vorhanden sey, wenn gleich nicht alle Verhältnisse aller
möglichen Theile bey zweyen Dingen einerley sind" (AN, 4,
p. 113). The Ninth Paragraph of his study is decisive and we
cite it here in its entirety.

> Da zu einer Aehnlichkeit nicht mehr erfodert
> wird, als dass die Theile des Bildes und die
> Verhältniss derselben nur im Absehen auf eine
> gewisse Beschaffenheit mit den Theilen des
> Vorbildes und der Verhältniss desselben einerley
> seyn müssen; da über dieses die wesentlichen
> Verhältnisse der Theile in dem Subject des Bildes
> vielerley Beschaffenheiten seyn, in deren

> Absicht die Theile des Bildes nicht einerley
> Verhältniss mit den Theilen des Vorbildes haben.
> Und das Bild kann dennoch dabey seine Aehnlichkeit
> mit dem Vorbilde haben (AN, 9, p. 120).

"Similarity", then, is not synonymous with "perfect agreement",
but implies variance from the original. It is with the nature
of this variance that Schlegel is primarily concerned. Indeed,
something may actually be added to the representation or image
("Bild") which is similar to, but not inherent in the object
itself. And it is this consistent inconsistency which excites
and pleases the beholder of a work of art.

Although without direct reference, Schlegel surely draws
upon Alexander Baumgarten for one of his basic tenets;
namely, the necessity of distinct perceptions ("deutliche
Begriffe") in the production of works of art (AN, 13, p.
125)[55]. "Nachahmen" is here equated with "poetisch beschreiben"
which implies far more than the mere reflection of the most
obvious features of an object.

> Aber ein Poet kann sie [die Dinge der Natur]
> niemals nachahmen, oder wie man es ordentlich
> nennet, poetisch beschreiben, wenn er nicht
> die Eigenschaften derselben von einander
> unterscheidet, und wenn er nicht mehr von einer
> Sache weis [sic] als dass es eine Blume, ein Thier
> oder dergleichen ist (AN, p. 125).

Curiously enough, a poem by Gottsched (which we cite later)
and another by Haller serve as illustrations of this trans-
ference of distinct perceptions to the art of poetry (AN,
p. 126).

Schlegel concludes the first part of his essay by referring to the order ("Ordnung", esp. AN , p. 126) which results
from clarity of perception. And it is the perception of this

order and of the similarity between the image and the
original by the reader which is said to arouse pleasure (AN,
15, p. 129).

> 2.   "Von den Eigenschaften und Regeln der
>   Nachahmung, in so weit ihr Endzweck
>   das Vergnügen ist"

In the second part of his essay, Schlegel addresses himself both to the ultimate purpose and to the proper objects of
imitation.

For Schlegel, the primary end of poetry is not instruction,
but the arousal of pleasure. His basic tenet is "dass Vergnügen dem Unterrichten vorgehe, und dass ein Dichter, der
vergnüget und nicht unterrichtet, als ein Dichter, höher zu
schätzen sey, als derjenige, der unterrichtet und nicht vergnüget" (AN, p. 135). Or, as he stated already in 1740 in his
Schreiben an den Herrn N. N. über die Comödie in Versen:
"Da das Vergnügen, welches man aus der Nachahmung empfindet,
der Endzweck ist, warum wir die Natur nachahmen, so verfehlt
die Nachahmung ihres Zweckes, so bald dieses Vergnügen auf-
höret."[56] It is this emphasis upon the arousal of pleasure
which results in a new rule of imitation ("Regel der Nachahmung").

> Suche so viel Vergnügen zu erwecken, als dein
> Vorbild und die Art der Nachahmung, und die jenigen,
> für die du nachahmest, zulassen (AN, p. 140).

This maxim has a profound effect on the proper objects of
imitation, as well. No longer were the originals to be sought
exclusively in nature. The Vorbild to be imitated was "der

Begriff und die Vorstellung von der Sache" (<u>AN</u>, p. 144). The
artistic representation, then, was to correspond to the perceptions which the beholder of art possessed of natural objects
and occurrences. Speaking as an artist, Schlegel concludes
"dass wir wissen, für wen wir nachahmen, damit wir uns die
Beschaffenheit dererjenigen, die wir vergnügen wollen, zu
Nutze machen und sie gleichsam auf ihrer empfindlichsten Seite
rühren können" (<u>AN</u>, 19, p. 140). For order and similarity will
not please, if the beholder has a different conception of the
object.

The fact nevertheless remains that our perceptions of
objects oftentimes vary from those of others. This does not
seem to bother Schlegel, however, primarily because of his
definition of the law of correspondence. An object may be
perceived differently, but since absolute correspondence in
imitation is not required in order to please, it is sufficient
if at least some aspect of the image is familiar to the beholder. From this it follows, "dass man zuweilen der Sache, die
man nachahmet, unähnlich werden muss, um <u>wohl</u> [well, i.e.
skillfully and pleasingly] nachzuahmen" (<u>AN</u>, p. 146) [italics
mine]. This is clearly expressed in the Twenty-First
Paragraph.

> Dinge, die an sich selbst einander nicht
> ähnlich sind, können sich einander ähnlich
> vorstellen, wenn man nämlich von dem einen
> oder dem andern eine andre Vorstellung hat,
> als es in der That beschaffen ist...Es geht
> aber dieses ebenfalls an, wenn das Bild nicht
> nur der Sache, sondern auch dem Begriffe, den
> man von der Sache zu haben pflegt, ganz
> ungleich ist. Denn ein solches Bild kann

> dennoch gut seyn, wenn es nur unter gewissen
> Umständen einen Eindruck in unsre Einbildungs-
> kraft macht, der dem Vorbilde gleich kömmt
> (<u>AN</u>, 21, p. 146).

Yet, as was true of his earlier essay, any dissimilarity must
go undetected, if it is to be successful (<u>AN</u>, p. 147). The
interrelatedness of Schlegel's two essays is thereby noted. It
is in the imagination of the <u>beholder</u> that the image is compared to the original (<u>AN</u>, 22, p. 148). And it is to this
faculty that the artistic imitation must appeal.

This does not mean, however, that every artistic image is
familiar to the beholder. Another object of imitation, then,
is that which is unfamiliar ("unbekannt") and new ("neu") (<u>AN</u>,
p. 151). It is therefore incumbent upon the <u>artist</u> to arouse
that conception within the mind of the beholder. And there are
at least three ways of achieving this. The first is to offer
essentially two descriptions, the one of the object to be
imitated, and the other of the secondary features or circum-
stances which may facilitate a clearer conception of the
imitated object. When the artist, for example, wishes to
imitate the actions of a hero, he should also offer a description of that hero's characteristics, so that he becomes
familiar to the beholder. A second way is to inform the beholder by associating the object with some characteristics
already known to him. Finally, and most importantly, the
artist has recourse to allegorical representation. Such representation assumes the place of the original while at the
same time projecting an image of an entirely different object.

To Schlegel's mind, such use of allegory results in twice as much order and, therefore, twice as much pleasure (AN, pp. 151-52)!

Much like Breitinger, Schlegel desires that the effect of art be as powerful as that of nature. His specific concern, however, is with the arousal of true passion ("wirkliche Leidenschaften"), rather than that of mere impressions ("blosse Einbildungen") (AN, p. 154). However, Schlegel is not very specific as to how this is to be achieved. Generally, he advises that the artist is free to use any means to arouse pleasure, as long as these means remain distinct. Furthermore, the artist must at all times remain sensitive toward the beholder's "Empfindung der Aehnlichkeit" (AN, pp. 134, 154). For, "alles Vergnügen gehört zu den Sachen, die man um ihrer selbst willen sucht" (AN, p. 134). The problem of defining just what constitutes that sensation, however, is conveniently avoided.

Most important to the moving of the beholder is a poetic, or "geblümte Schreibart" (AN, p. 159). "Zweydeutigkeit", "der ungewisse Ausdruck" (AN, p. 138), and "die Mattigkeit in einem Gedichte", i.e. "ein Mangel derjenigen Dinge, welche die Bilder in der Einbildungskraft lebhaft machen" (AN, p. 139) are to be avoided. What Schlegel recommends is extensive clarity and vivid imagery (Baumgarten), and, again, it is the same poem by Gottsched, alluded to earlier, which serves as the best illustration of this type of poetic style:

> Schaue, wie sich Haupt und Glied
> Fleisch und Bein so künstlich fügen,
> Wie sich Flächs und Sehne zieht,
> Wie die vollen Muskeln liegen.
> Gieb auf deiner Adern Menge
> Und des Blutes Kreislauf acht,
> Den das Herz mit reger Macht
> Durch sein spritzendes Gedränge,
> In die kleinsten Zäsern treibt,
> Dass kein Pünktchen saftlos bleibt.

So it is through clarity of speech and vividness of imagery that imitation is capable of moving the beholder of art.

In Gottsched's poetic theory, there is a balance between the instructive and the pleasurable aspects of art. For Breitinger, who stands very much under the influence of the rhetorical tradition and the Frenchman Dubos, the moving of the beholder is the primary function of literature. In Schlegel's aesthetic theory, however, the arousal of pleasure and passion becomes the foremost end of art.

In our reassessment of poetic imitation at the time of the early German Aufklärung, we have come to understand that these critics, and artists in their own right, far from suggesting any sort of photographic reproduction of reality, actually encouraged what we have termed the "creative imitation of nature."

Gottsched's call for indirect instruction and the free invention of plot, i.e. for "eine unter gewissen Umständen mögliche, aber nicht würcklich vorgefallene Begebenheit, darunter eine nützliche moralische Wahrheit verborgen liegt", reveals the true nature of his theory of imitation. For Gottsched, the essence of art consists in the delicate, i.e.

artistic balance between verisimilitude and creativity in the imitation of nature.

Beginning with the idea that the poet is essentially another creator, Breitinger, although careful to retain verisimilitude, further develops this idea of creative imitation by exploring the nature of the world of the possible and by focusing upon the forces of nature.

The poet is no longer seen as a creative imitator of all natural things, but rather as an imitator of the art of God. The literary artist is now endowed with the power to create new and possible worlds which leave a lasting effect on the beholder. Literature therefore becomes a dynamic form of creative expression.

With respect to the theories of imitation as outlined by Gottsched and Breitinger, W. Bender's assertion that the two poetologists are basically united on this point is a valid one. "Die eigentlich neue Akzentsetzung liegt in der Erweiterung- nicht in der Überwindung- des herkömmlichen Nachahmungsprinzips durch die Einbeziehung nicht nur der wirklichen, sondern auch der möglichen Welten".[57] By making the creation of new and possible worlds the very center of his poetics, Breitinger reveals the very heart of artistic expression and subsequently goes far beyond Gottsched.

However, where Gottsched and Breitinger had failed to reconcile the call for the law of correspondence in their emphasis upon the creative imitation of nature, Johann Elias Schlegel defined most clearly the relationship between the

artistic representation and the original. J.E. Schlegel was
the first, then, to state that the mere <u>appearance</u> of similarity
is oftentimes sufficient to poetic imitation, and that as long
as this semblance of correspondence is enticing enough to
maintain the attention of the beholder, that such consistent
inconsistency can be justified.[58] Poetic imitations, in
Schlegel's understanding, should correspond, not only to the
actual original in nature ("Urbild"), but to the concept or
image ("Vorbild") which the beholder possesses of the natural
object[59]. Poetic imitations, then, may at times be quite
dissimilar in comparison with the actual phenomenon.

Already, then, at the time of the early German <u>Aufklärung</u>,
the law of correspondence had been seriously challenged. The
limits of creative imitation had been extended. What at first
had been a suggestion by Opitz, namely, that the poet should
imitate not what is but what could or should be, now became the
very essence of the imitation theory in the early 18th Century.
And far more room was given to the creative imagination than
seemed to at first meet the eye. With J. E. Schlegel's
insistence that the artist must imitate ideas and images,
either his own or that of the beholder of art, we encounter,
already in 1741 and 1742, the beginning of what may be termed
an internalization or subjectivization of the imitation theory
which reaches its height in Sturm und Drang:

> Die Poesie scheint sich dadurch von allen
> Künsten und Wissenschaften zu unterscheiden,
> dass sie diese beiden Quellen [die Nachahmung
> der Natur und das Anschauen] vereinigt, alles

> scharf durchdacht, durchforscht, durchschaut-
> und dann in getreuer Nachahmung zum andermal
> wieder hervorgebracht".[60]

Indeed, by concentrating on the imitation of the idea which one

possesses of the natural object, there is a definite shift

from the world of phenomena to the world of noumena. From

here, it is but one easy step from the theory of imitation to

the almost exclusive concentration upon the power of the

creative imagination to create a world of its own--a step which

the German Romantics were to take at the turn of the new

century.[61]

CHAPTER II

CONCERNING THE IMAGINATION

> Der Poetische Enthusiasmus...
> jaget die Einbildungs-Krafft
> in eine ausserordentliche Hitze,
> und führet den Dichter gleichsam
> ausser sich selbst...(Bodmer).

I. Johann Jacob Bodmer's Concept of Einbildungs-Krafft

A. Imagination in the Discourse der Mahlern

In the Nineteenth Discourse (Part I) of the Discourse der Mahlern (1721), Bodmer ("Rubeen" as pseudonym) hails Opitz over all other German poets because of his ability to fill the imagination with fascinating objects (DM, I, pp. *2-3 of Disc. XIX.) and concludes that imagination informed by passion is the key to art:

> Wen auf diese Weise die Imagination von der
> Passion begleitet wird, alsdann ist sie im
> Stande sich ohne Distraction über ein Objekte
> aufzuhalten, und sich die Natur Gestalt und
> Grösse desselben bekandt zumachen; Und dieses
> ist die Manier, die sie braucht, sich
> auszuschmücken und zu bereichern (DM, I, p. *4
> of Disc. XIX.).

Hence, only a poet such as Opitz who enriches his art with vibrant imagery "kan lebhafft und natürlich dichten" (DM, I, p. *4 of Disc. XIX.). As we shall see time and again, naturalness means liveliness of expression.

The creative imagination is perceived here, however, as an

essentially _reproductive faculty, in that it recalls to the
mind those sensations and impressions which had been aroused
upon the first encounter with the object (DM, I, p. *4 of Disc.
XIX.).

> Dieselbe wird alle die Affec[t]e die ihn schon
> besessen haben, in ihm wider rege machen, und
> ihm davon erhitzen, nicht anderst als wen er
> sie wirklich in der Brust fühlte (DM, I, p. *4
> of Disc. XIX.).

If, for instance, one were resting and reflecting under a shady
oak tree, all those sensations could be recalled to mind by
simply exercising one's imagination:

> ...so bringet ihm doch die Stärcke seiner
> Imagination alle die Ideen wieder zurück,
> die er gehabt ·hat, als er wircklich verliebt,
> mitleidend, betrübt, erzörnt gewesen, sie
> setzet ihn in einen eben so hitzigen Stande,
> als er damahlen gestanden ware, und ruffet
> ihm dieselbe Expressionen wieder zurück,
> welcher er sich zur selben Zeit bedienet
> (DM, I, p. *5 of XIX. Disc.).

Von Besser (1654-1729), for example, is said to write
poetry which reflects "die reichste Imagination" and which
contains the most lively of descriptions (DM, I, p. *5 cf XIX.
Disc.). Indeed, for Bodmer, the elegies ("Klag-Gedichte") of
Besser and Friedrich Rudolf von Canitz (1654-1699) which were
written upon the loss of their wives· constitute "die zwey
passionierteste Stücke, welche wir in der Deutschen Poesie
haben" (DM, I, p. *6 of XIX. Disc.). And the power of attraction generated by these poems lies in their deeply moving content and style. "Es ist unmöglich, dass ein Leser nicht einen
Theil der Grösse des Affectes, welcher sie beyde erhitzet hat,

in seinem Hertzen empfinde" (<u>DM</u>, I, p. *6 of XIX. Disc.).
Such "Stärcke der Passion" (<u>DM</u>, I. p. *7 of XIX. Disc.)
surely reveals "dass Amor ihnen ihre Verse in die Feder ge-
flösset hat" (<u>DM</u>, I, p. *8 of XIX. Disc.). It is their
"Enthusiasmum", "Inspiration", and "Poetische Raserey" which
excites and moves the beholder (<u>DM</u>, I, p. *8 of XIX. Disc.),
and such poetic madness, as it were, is the key to a powerfully
effective poetry.

> Wenn er [der Poet] also erhitzet ist, so wachsen
> ihm, so zusagen, die Worte auf der Zungen, er
> beschreibet nichts als was er siehet, er redet
> nichts, als was er empfindet, er wird von der
> Passion fortgetrieben, nicht anderst als ein
> Rasender, der ausser sich selbst ist, und
> folgen muss, wohin ihn seine Raserey führet
> (<u>DM</u>, I, p. *8 of XIX. Disc.).

In Part III, the Twenty-First Discourse (1722), the writer
("Holbein") recapitulates what Bodmer had maintained earlier.
The poet's imagination is here described in terms of its
affinity to painting. The imagination paints images of things
and projects them onto the mind of the beholder. Figuratively
speaking, the imagination of the reader becomes "der Plan oder
das Feld, auf welchem er seine Gemählde entwirft" (<u>DM</u>, III,
p. 163, XXI, Disc.). The artist's quill becomes "der Pinsel,
mit dem er in dieses grosse Feld der Imagination mahlet", and
words are compared to "Farben, die er so wol zu vermischen,
zu erhöhen, zu verdunckeln und auszutheilen weiss, dass ein
jeder Gegenstand in derselben seine lebhafte und natürliche
Gestalt gewinnet" (<u>DM</u>, III, p. 164, XXI. Disc.). The poet,
then, is "ein curieuser Mahler, der durch blosse Worte ein

Gemähide verfertiget:..." (DM, III, p. 164, XXI. Disc.).
The best painter is· one who creates the ·most lively images,
"dass wir wie in einen Zweifel gerathen, ob wir nicht das
Original selbst vor den Augen sehen" (DM, III, p. 164, XXI.
Disc.). In like fashion, the best poet is the one "der seinen
Lesern solche lebhaffte Bildnisse in die Imagination mahlen
kann, dass sie die Originale darinne wie auf einer Taffel oder
in einem Spiegel sehen" (DM, III, pp. 164-165, XXI. Disc.).
Desiring, then, to communicate his ideas to others, an author
"setzet sich vor in ihre Imagination eben diejenigen Schildereyen zu copiren, die in seinem Kopf gemahlet sind" (DM, III,
p. 167, XXI. Disc.).

It is poetic enthusiasm which accounts for the liveliness
of poetry, but sensible judgment which retains order and
naturalness of expression. This is the balance which informs
the thought of all the early Aufklärer.

B. Von dem Einfluss und Gebrauche Der
Einbildungs-Kraft (1727)[1]

Bodmer is insofar a sensualist as he maintains that man
comes to an awareness of his existence by way of the senses
("unsere ersten Lehr-Meister" (VEK, p. 2)). Although it is
in the contemplation of objects that we come to know the
world which surrounds us, vivid impressions of that world
can only be received through immediate sensation and constant
observation. Only as long as we behold the object will it
retain its spell over us. As soon as it disappears, the clear

perception which we possessed of the object vanishes as well:
"...so offt sie [die Dinge] wieder aus den Sinnen rücken,
rücken auch die Begrieffe und Empfindungen, so sie gestifftet,
zugleich hinweg" (VEK, p. 3). Bodmer does not maintain that
our memory of the object is erased as soon as the object
disappears, but that it is the clear concept of the object itself which fades away. Memory, belonging to the lower grades
of knowledge, is simply not able to excite and move us like
the clear and vivid perception of an object. It becomes the
proper function of the imagination, therefore, to recall those
sensations and impressions which were experienced in our first
encounter with an object, even in the total absence of that
object. This is the first definition of Einbildungs-Krafft in
Bodmer's essay (VEK, p. 5).

The specific problem investigated by Bodmer is the relationship between imagination and sensation. The critic
maintains that the imagination possesses the equivalent power
to move us ("nicht minder starck rühren", VEK, p. 5) as the
sensation we experience while contemplating the actual object.
To use one of Bodmer's own examples, the experience of St.
Peter's Cathedral in Rome can be relived time and again by way
of the imagination, irrespective of our location grographically
(VEK, p. 5). Nonetheless, if it is the clear and vivid perception of an object which most effectively moves us, then
we must ask ourselves how the imagination, which does not contain clarity of perception, can possibly be as powerful as
that of sensation?

Bodmer admits that the images of the imagination are not as distinct ("nicht·so deutlich") as the' perceptions of sensation ("Empfindung"). Yet, he insists that these images can obtain a great measure of clarity ("einen grossen Zusatz von Klarheit"), if only the imagination is allowed to operate alone, without interference from the senses (VEK, p. 6). With this insight, a far greater appreciation for the autonomy of the creative imagination was to be won than critics have cared to admit.[2]

Furthermore, with the assistance of prolonged observation and constant practice in the discernment of the individual features and characteristics of an object, one can attain distinctness of perception ("Deutlichkeit") and thereby begin to rival the power which sensation generates (VEK, p. 7).

As for the arousal of pleasure, the law of correspondence, of complete agreement between the artistic representation and its original, when heeded, could serve as a powerful source of pleasure (VEK, pp. 10, 15, 23, 29-30), for appearance is compared to actuality in the mind of the beholder. In our capacity as judges ("Richter", VEK, p. 30), then, we are flattered, pleased and, without our knowing, instructed.

> Also merken wir nicht, dass der Verfasser
> uns unterrichten wollen; sondern glauben
> vielmehr, dass er die Demuth gehabt habe,
> seine Gemählde uns zu unserer Beurtheilung
> zu übergeben, welches unsern Hochmuth
> angenehm kitzelt. Mithin eignen wir uns
> eine Herrschafft über den Verfasser an
> (VEK, p. 30).

For "wir lassen uns gerne auf eine so angenehme Weise betriegen"

(<u>VEK</u>, p. 31).

It does not take the critic long to consider the merits of the imagination for the writing of literature.

> Wenn die Einbildungs-Krafft so reichlich
> angefüllt ist, so muss sie notwendig
> einen herrlichen Einfluss über eine Schrift
> haben, indem sie dieselbe mit lebhafften
> Bildnissen und Gemählden belebet, welche
> den Leser gleichsam bezaubern; Er vergisst
> darüber, dass er nur die Beschreibungen
> der Sachen lieset, und fällt auf den Wahn,
> er sehe die Dinge selber vor sich, und
> wohne den erzehlten Begebenheiten versöhnlich
> bey (<u>VEK</u>, p. 9).

Bodmer's essay is the first in-depth study of the creative imagination in the history of German poetics and aesthetics, and thus warrants a far more detailed analysis than has been rendered in the past.

For Bodmer, it is from careful and continual observation of the originals ("Urbilder") in nature that the imagination draws its greatest strength: "dieselbe schwellet sie auf, und treibet sie in eine ausserordentliche Hitze, nicht anderst als der Wind das Feuer" (<u>VEK</u>, p. 16). And just as this creative frenzy reaches a feverish pitch, it is channeled through the medium of language and given definite form.

> ...Also muss ein Schreiber vor allen Dingen
> seine Sprache wol verstehen; er muss die
> Macht, welche in den verschiedenen Worten
> einer Sprache lieget, wol erwogen haben;...
> Er muss Verstand und Urtheil haben, zu
> erkennen, welcher Ausdruck am bequemsten
> seye, einen Begrieff darein zu kleiden,
> und auf seinen besten Vortheil auszuschmücken
> (<u>VEK</u>, p. 18).

So it is precisely through language that the effect which the artistic representation has upon the beholder is able to rival the impression which the natural object leaves with the observor. Necessary therefore to a successful, i.e. power- fully effective work of art, are an "erhitzte Einbildungs- Krafft", "eine gute Kundschaft der Sprach [e]" (VEK, p. 24), and an "erhabene Schreib-Art" (VEK, p. 25). These are the chief means by which the reader derives pleasure ("Belustigung"), i.e. "dass wir zugleich entzündet und erleuchtet werden" (VEK, p. 27).

It is Bodmer's deepest conviction "dass eine feuerige Einbildungs-Krafft vermögend seye die Gegenstände, wenn sie gleich abwesend, so lebendig vor das Gesicht zu stellen, dass das Gemüthe unterschiedlich beweget wird, und eben die jenige Leidenschafften in unsrer Brust entbrennen, welche der Gegenstand, wenn er anwesend ist, durch die Sinnen erregen kan" (VEK, pp. 118-119). The primary function of the poet is to pleasantly move the reader. And this can best be accomplished by "eine wolgeübte und lebhaffte Einbildungs-Krafft" (VEK, p. 119).

Consistent with his method of supporting theoretical pro- nouncements with concrete examples, Bodmer again cites those two poems which, "in den Schrifften unsrer Deutschen Poesie", he considers the most moving ("die beweglichsten")--those of Canitz and Besser[3]. Although varying in their treatment of lost love, both are found to be "hertzrührend" and "natürlich" (VEK, p. 124)--the two most repeated adjectives used by Bodmer in his literary criticism when speaking of good poetry. The real key, however, to the success of these poems is the personal experience which has informed them.

> Wenn wir denen Ursachen nachspühren wollen,
> warum diese beyden Gedichte so wol gerathen;
> so ist keine andere, als weil diese beyde
> Poeten ihre eigene Noth, die sie so empfindtlich
> gerührt hat, beklagen (VEK, p. 131).

What Bodmer is actually praising, then, is a poetry based in experience--an early call for what is essentially "Erlebnis-dichtung". It is not observation alone (Brockes, Haller), but personal experience (Canitz, Besser) which receives the highest praise here.

Since the proper end of poesy is "die wahre Bildung des Gemüthes" (VEK, p. 199), the artist must combine an exact knowledge of human psychology with an eloquent and moving style.

Besides recommending the works of Christian Wolff (particularly his Gedancken von der Menschen Thun und Lassen (1720) (VEK, p. 184)), to whom the present work is dedicated, and the Roman, Sallustius, (VEK, p. 185) for instruction into human behavior, Bodmer continually emphasizes the importance of personal experience and observation. This knowledge of man can be acquired through study of the external manifestations of emotion, for "die Affecten...verrathen sich durch deutliche Merckmahle" (VEK, p. 97). One such sign is that of human gestures.

> Gleich wie die Mahlerey die Sprache der
> Imagination ist, und die Worte die Sprache
> der Gedancken sind, also sind die Grimatzen
> eine gewisse Sprache, durch welche sich
> die Passionen ausdrücken (DM, IV, Disc.
> XIII, p. *2)

Or, as explained in the present essay:

> Was die Worte den Gedancken sind, das sind
> die Gebehrden den Leidenschafften, ihre
> Zeugen und Dollmetschen. Die Natur selbst
> hat den Menschen diese Sprache der
> Leidenschafften gelehrt; dahero sie allen
> Völckern gemeine und bekannt (VEK, p. 99).

Most important, however, for an effectively moving literature is
an intense study of speech and figures of speech, for inasmuch
as "die Gemüths-Bewegungen einen grossen Einfluss über die
Zunge haben" (VEK, p. 99), it is obvious that a study of
language will reveal the nature of human emotions. Bodmer
maintains therefore that each passion speaks its own language
(VEK, p. 109). And it was the classical rhetoricians who first
named these signs, 'figures of speech' ("Figurn der Rede und
der Worten", VEK, p. 109), or 'schemes of construction'.

In his essay, Bodmer discusses such intensive linguistic
study in terms of its end: the revelation of human nature.
This is summed up in "eine allgemeine Regel":

> ...Dass der gantze Inhalt derselben aus der
> Natur der Dingen und der Menschen gleichsam
> heraus gesponnen werde, dergestalt, dass die
> Sitten dessen, der redet, deutlich aus seinen
> Reden hervor brechen und daraus zu erkennen
> seyen. Hieraus erhellet, dass, wer der
> gleichen Reden verfertigen will, vor allen
> Dingen die Natur derer Eigenschafften oder
> den Character derer Personen, die er
> einführen will, fleissig studieren und sich
> auf das genaueste bekant machen müsse
> (VEK, p. 200).

Through study of the moral character of man, that is, by ob-
serving "die freyen Handlungen", which are either good or bad,
"je nachdem sie dem Gesetze der Natur gemäss oder entgegen
sind" (VEK, p. 147), the artist has access to one of the

"deutlichsten Merckzeichen, durch welche der innere Zustand des Gemüthes sich zu erkennen giebt" (VEK, p. 147).

We cannot emphasize enough Bodmer's concern for the power of the artist to move his audience. Through intensive study of human nature, the artist will be able not only to differentiate between emotions, but to determine the degree of their intensity ("Stärcke", VEK, p. 110). And through "die Beobachtung der passionierten Personen", the way is prepared "zu einer Kundschafft der mannigfaltigen Sprach-Arten der Regungen" (VEK, pp. 111-112). The key to moving the beholder, however, is by informing poetry with personal experience, "wenn er [the artist] selbst von denen Regungen gerührt ist, die er ihnen [the audience] erregen will" (VEK, p. 118). And it is by way of the creative imagination that the artist can excite and move the beholder. For it is the peculiar power of the imagination that it can present before the audience, not only forgotten impressions, but the exciting and moving experience itself which had accompanied the perception of such phenomena. It is for the purpose of moving and exciting the beholder that the creative imagination must be "fiery". Observation and experience combine to skillfully and clearly portray the action in a work of art, in order that the beholder may be most powerfully affected.

> Wer des Menschen Natur kennt, dem ist
> unverborgen, dass die Affecten, die
> nichts anders sind, als eine undeutliche
> Vorstellung des Guten und Bösen, die
> meisten mahle von der Einbildungs-Krafft
> aus ihrem Schlaffe aufgeweckt und
> determinirt werden. Wenn denn eine

wolgeübte und lebhaffte Einbildungs-
Krafft durch deutliche Vorstellungen
in eine biegsame empfindtliche Seele
wirket, die leicht Feuer fängt, so kan
das Gemüth nicht ungestört in seiner Ruhe
bleiben; sondern es wird, je nachdem der
Gegenstand beschaffen ist, welchen es
durch einen unvermerckten Betrug der
Einbildungs-Krafft gegenwertig siehet
und wircklich empfindet, entweder mit
einem sanften Ergötzen, oder Furcht
und Schrecken, oder Erbarmen, oder Zorn
und Eyfer erfüllt: Welche innerliche
Regungen dann nicht in dem Gemüthe
verborgen liegen bleiben; sondern sich
alsobald in den Minen und Gebehrden, wie
auch in der Rede hervor thun. Auf diese
Weise kan ein Schreiber, der eine reiche
Einbildungs-Krafft und eine zarte und
rege Seele besitzet, Leidenschafften
annehmen, wenn und wie er will (VEK, p. 119).

Bodmer, while drawing directly on Longinus' On the

Sublime--an act which signals a turn from the concept of judg-

ment as a thing of rule to a thing of taste[4]--called for the

necessity of poetic enthusiasm à la Plato. For it is poetic

enthusiasm which ignites creative imagination.

Der Poetische Enthusiasmus ist nichts anders,
als die äusserst starcke Leidenschafft, womit
das gantze Gemüth eines Authors für seine
Materie eingenommen und angefüllet ist, diese
bindet die äussern Sinnen, dass sie von denen
umstehenden Dingen nicht gerühret werden; sie
jaget die Einbildungs-Krafft in eine ausserordentliche Hitze, und führet den Dichter
gleichsam ausser sich selbst, dass er die
Einbildungen von den Empfindungen nicht
unterscheiden kan,...sondern meinet er sehe
und fühle die Dinge gegenwärtig (VEK, p. 238).

Indeed, Bodmer even goes so far as to suggest that this source

of inspiration may at times be so powerful as to lead to re-

velation. The "Einbildungs-Krafft alleine" may display such

a "prophetische Krafft" (VEK, p. 238), "dass den Dichtern,

wenn ihre Einbildungs-Krafft durch eine starcke Leidenschafft
angeflammet ist, das Zukünfftige, so sie wünschen und verlangen
gleichsam in dem Bilde vor dem Gesicht schwebet" (VEK, p. 239).

The special power of the imagination, however, lies in
its capacity to make the beholder of art believe in the
occurrences which move before him. It is this "währende [r]
Irrthum" (VEK, p. 239) which Bodmer encourages.

> Dieses ist so viel als der äusserste Schwung,
> den sich eine belebte Einbildungs-Krafft
> geben kan, und von solchem Nachdruck, dass es
> scheinet, als ob sie sich selbst übersteigen
> wolle, und ist kein Wunder, wenn dergleichen
> sich nur zur Seltenheit ereignen, weil sie
> von einer äusserst erhitzten Neigung allein
> können gestifftet werden (VEK, p. 239).

And it is the poetry of Canitz, Opitz and Pietsch which serves
as the best example of "eine belebte Einbildungs-Krafft" at
work.

It is the proper function of "dieser Schwung der
Einbildungs-Krafft" to enliven those descriptions, "welche
das Hertze rühren und bewegen sollen" (VEK, p. 246). This is
the ultimate end of literary works of art.

C. Anklagung Des verderbten Geschmackes, Oder
   Critische Anmerkungen Uber Den Hamburgischen
   Patrioten, Und Die Hallischen Tadlerinnen (1728)[5]

Bodmer's critical assault on two of the major moral
weeklies of the day is dedicated to that first defender of good
taste in Germany, Johann Ulrich König (1688-1744).

Most important for our consideration here are Bodmer's
pronouncements concerning the creative imagination in Section E

of his work, entitled, "Von den Dichtungen überhaupt". In

obvious anticipation of Breitinger's formulation of the world

of the possible, Bodmer, twelve years in advance, exclaims:

> ...ein Scribent bauet sich selbst in seiner
> erhitzten Phantasey neue Welten, die er mit
> neuen Einwohnern bevölkert, welche von einer
> andern Natur sind und eigenen Gesetzen folgen
> (AVG, p. 110).

The poet, then,

> ...dichtet sich neue Personen und neue
> Begegnissen: Bald giebet er den Todten
> das Leben wieder und verbindet sie in
> allerley Unterredungen;...bald giebt er
> den Fablen und Mährchen einen grossen
> Schein der Wahrheit;...Aber alle diese
> und andere dergleichen Arten von Dichtungen
> sind allein erfunden worden...Und es ist
> diese Freyheit der Dichtung nicht ohne
> Gesetze: dann sonst müsste man alle
> Träumereyen und Wähne verrückter Sinne für
> geistreich und scharffsinnig erklähren
> (AVG, pp. 110-111). [emphasis mine]

At this point, Bodmer wishes only to cite a few "Grund-

Regeln" and postpone treatment of "alle Grund-Regeln der

Dichtung in ihrer ordentlichen Verknüpfung" for his "vor-

habendes grosses Werk", a work which never materialized.

For Bodmer, the purpose of poesy is, "dass sie auf eine

ergötzende Art unterrichte" (AVG, p. 111). Poesy must be

"wahrscheinlich". It must either be based on actual and

similar events, or at least be consistent with "einen

angenommenen allgemeinen Wahn" (AVG, p. 112). Most striking,

however, is the insistence that poesy must have "einen

Mystischen Sinn" (AVG, p. 112).

> Alle figürliche Umstände der Dichtung
> müssen ihre besondere Bedeutung haben,

die den Mystischen Sinn des ganzen Systematis
vollkommen machen (<u>AVG</u>, p. 112).

What is called for is correspondence between "de [m] erdichteten
Systematis" and "de [m] Mystischen Systematis" (<u>AVG</u>, p. 112),
that is, between the invented representation and the deeper
meaning of the work itself. This serves as one of the main
criteria in the literary analysis of poetry in Bodmer's critical
essays.

In Part III of Section E, "Von den Träumen und Gesichtern",
Bodmer discusses those "Poetische Träume", which, unlike
everyone's dreams, "nothwendig ihre Regeln und Gesetze zu
beobachten haben, welche der Ausgelassenheit der Fantasie
Ziel und Maasse se [t] zen, jedoch einem Dichter ungleich
mehrere Freyheit geben, als er hatte nehmen dörffen, so er
wachend geschrieben hätte" (<u>AVG</u>, pp. 134-135). Consistent with
Bodmer's earlier essay (1727) is the insight that "die Fantasie",
which transports us from one scene to another, "setzet uns in
den Genuss der höchsten Glückseligkeit; sie erschaffet neue
Wesen; sie verwandelt uns" (<u>AVG</u>, p. 135). The creative
imagination, then, although bound by certain rules, obviously
gains a new freedom in Bodmer's critical essay.

Nonetheless, although Bodmer ascribes to the creative
imagination a great deal of freedom, this faculty is never
allowed to transcend the limits of logic. "Aber, so eine
grosse Zauberin sie gleich ist, kan sie doch nicht streitende
Dinge machen, die sich selbst widersprechen..." (<u>AVG</u>, p. 135).

In sum, it is striking how much creative freedom Bodmer

grants to the poet. Once more we are led to ask ourselves
what Bodmer's position is with respect to the creative potential
of the imagination.

As we have seen, his thoughts on the creative imagination
in the 1720's reflect a striking vacillation between limited
reproduction, on the one hand, and creative frenzy, on the
other.

Common to the Discourse der Mahlern and his essay, Von
dem Einfluss und Gebrauche der Einbildungs-Krafft, is the idea
that the main function of the imagination is to recall forgotten·
impressions. The imagination, therefore, is perceived as a
primarily reproductive faculty. Understood as such, it is
limited in its creative potential. In the Anklagung Des
verderbten Geschmacks, however, the "erhitzte Phantasey" is
visualized as the faculty which creates new worlds which operate
in accordance with their own laws. Poetry therefore gains a
new freedom.

Bodmer's thoughts on the creative imagination thus under-
go a certain transformation already in the 1720's. In this
transformation one can discern a line of development which
leads from the Discourse der Mahlern to Breitinger's Critische
Dichtkunst and the postulation of the virtual autonomy of the
Einbildungskraft as a creative and practically self-sufficient
faculty.

Bodmer also perceives that the poetry of this period is
imbued with a new vitality. At the same time, Bodmer's presuppositions with respect to what constitutes good poetry

are revealed in his literary analyses. Good poetry must be "lebhaft", "hertzrührend" and "natürlich". And it is the poetry of Opitz, Canitz, and Besser which serves as the model for Bodmer.

This spontaneity of poetic expression, Bodmer attributes to what he terms "poetische Raserey". This seemingly divine madness is the true source of inspiration for the creative artist. In this way, poetry was to be infused with a new energy which, it was hoped, would lead to an expansion of the power of the poet to create freely and spontaneously from within. This is the true beginning of the subjectivization of art which eventually culminated in German Romanticism. The creative imagination was now "erhitzt", "belebt", "feuerig" and "angeflammet" by poetic enthusiasm.

Yet, there were definite limitations to the creativity of the imagination. Creative imagination was also to be "wolgeübt", which implied that it was free to create only within the bounds of reasonableness, i.e. within the limits of probability. As Bodmer states in the Anklagung Des verderbten Geschmacks, what is probable may be based on a generally accepted illusion or belief ("Wahn"). As long as the illusions which the poet creates in his work correspond to the idea in the mind of the beholder of what is probable, then that is sufficient to art. This expansion of the limits of probability thus opened up new vistas for the creative play of the imagination.

The actual thrust of Bodmer's thoughts in these early essays is toward the moving of the beholder of art. It is for this reason that Bodmer insists that "Einbildungen" become as strong as sensations. And, as we shall 'see, this ambition was common to Gottsched, Baumgarten and Breitinger, as well. This is also why the poet was required to first study the inner workings of the human heart. For in order to move one needs to know how one is best moved. And both observation (the cognitive) and experience (the sensual) supply such knowledge. By being moved oneself, one is able to create heart-stirring images which set our soul in motion.

Poetic enthusiasm sparks creative imagination which creates images ("Einbildungen") and a new world which operates in accordance with its own laws. This is the "Freyheit der Dichtung" (AVG, p. 111). Bodmer's thoughts on the creative imagination reflect a balance between poetic enthusiasm and sensible judgment, although his thought tends to lean toward the creation of a new freedom of expression.

II. Gottsched on the Imagination

A. Einbildungskraft in the Critische Dichtkunst

Like Bodmer before him, Gottsched insists that the genuine artist must be acutely aware of human behavior. Through diligent study of nature, the poet is able to perceive the inner workings of the heart.

> Vor allen Dingen ist einem wahren Dichter
> eine gründliche Erkenntnis des Menschen
> nöthig, ja ganz unentbehrlich. Ein Poet
> ahmet hauptsächlich die Handlungen der
> Menschen nach, die von ihrem freien Willen
> herrühren und vielmahls aus den verschiedenen
> Neigungen des Gemüths und hefftigen Affecten

> ihren Ursprung haben. Daher muss derselbe
> ja die Natur und Beschaffenheit des Willens,
> der sinnlichen Begierde, und des sinnlichen
> Abscheues in allen ihren mannigfaltigen
> Gestalten gründlich einsehen lernen...
> Der Poet muss also auch die Gemüths-Kräffte
> der vernünftigen Seele, und ihren verschiedenen,
> sowohl bösen als guten Gebrauch kennen; damit
> er thörichte Leute thöricht, und so ferner
> Abergläubische, Leichtgläubige, Ungläubige,
> Vernünftler, Grübler, Zweifler, Einfältige,
> Spitzfündige, Verschlagene, Dumme und Kluge
> nach ihrer gehörigen Art abzuschildern und
> nachzuahmen im Stande sey (VCD, p. 90).

The true poet cannot do without such knowledge of human

nature, of moral character, of the laws of Nature, and of

political events (VCD, p. 91). And this is necessary in order

for art to fulfill its twofold purpose of instructing and

pleasing the beholder.

Gottsched perceives of the poet as part maker and part

creator. This is made most explicit in the "Anmerckungen" to

Gottsched's translation of Horace's Ars poetica, where the

Leipzig professor discusses the question of whether natural

genius or the faithful observation of rules is most important

for the development of the genuine artist.

> Ingenium, Cicero im I. Buche vom Wahrsagen
> schreibt, Democritus habe davor gehalten,
> dass ohne die Raserey oder Begeisterung
> niemand ein grosser Poet seyn könne.
> Gewisser massen hat er recht. Aber wenn
> er von seinem Geiste die Regeln der Kunst
> und die Vernunft ausschliesst: so wird er
> lauter unsinnige Poeten auf dem Parnass
> haben wollen, wie Horatz spricht, excludit
> sanos Helicone Poetas: und Plato wird Recht
> haben, wenn er in seiner Republic keine
> Dichter leiden will. Indessen halten doch
> bis auf den heutigen Tag die meisten davor,
> die Poeten würden gebohren, und wüchsen
> gleichsam wie die Piltzen fix und fertig
> aus der Erden. Höchstens, meynen sie, man

> müsse sich die Regeln der Verssmacher-Kunst,
> vom scandiren und Reimen ein wenig bekannt
> machen: das übrige gebe sich von selbst.
> Wenn Pritschmeister Poeten wären, so hätten
> sie gantz recht (VCD, p. 37). [emphasis mine]

What Gottsched objects to here is not poetic enthusiasm, but

the lack of respect for the techne of artistic production.

Indeed, Gottsched never denies that poetic "Raserey" or

"Begeisterung" lies at the heart of the creative process, but

seriously questions the prevalent attitude of the day that

poets operate somehow irrespective of the principles of art and

reason. Our point becomes clearer a few pages later.

> Nichts ist bey jungen Leuten gewöhnlicher als
> diese Frage; zumahl wenn sie hören dass die
> Poeten nicht gemacht, sondern gebohren werden.
> Haben Sie nun etwa ein gutes Naturell zum
> Reimen: so bilden sie sich ein, sie brauchten
> nun keiner beschwerlichen Regeln mehr, als
> die doch ohne dem keinen Poeten machten. Sie
> schreiben also in den Tag hinein, und dichten
> auf ein gerathe wohl. Alle ihre Einfälle
> müssen gut, und alle Fehler lauter Orackel
> seyn. Andre, die kein Fünkchen natürlichen
> Witz besitzen, wollen alles aus Regeln
> lernen. Aber beyde fehlen, und Horatz hilft
> ihnen zurechte (VCD, pp. 48-49) [emphasis mine]

It is, therefore, this balance between creative exuberance and

adherence to the basic principles of artistic production which

most adequately characterizes Gottsched's concept of the poet.

Where Bodmer allows more room for poetic enthusiasm,

Gottsched maintains a strict balance between enthusiasm and

reasonable expression. This is most obvious in Gottsched's

rejection of Besser's poem which Bodmer had praised as one of

the two best poems of German origin. Besser's "Jammer"

dominates the poem in Gottsched's estimation and therefore up-

sets the delicate balance mentioned above. Gottsched
concludes:

> Der Affect hat bey dem Verluste einer
> ungemeinen Ehgattin, ungemein und
> wunderbar seyn sollen: Er ist aber
> unglaublich geworden...Besser hat als
> ein künstlicher Poet, nicht als ein
> trostloser Wittwer geweinet (VCD, p. 158).

This early disagreement is precursory to the later quarrel
between Leipzig and Zürich in the 1740's.

The creative imagination, as discussed in the Critische
Dichtkunst, is but one part of a greater structure of the mind
of the artist. Witz, Scharfsinnigkeit, and Einbildungs-Krafft
mutually cooperate to bring about a genuine work of art. "Alle
diese Gemüths-Kräffte nun, gehören in einem hohen Grade vor
denjenigen, der geschickt nachahmen soll" (VCD, p. 86).

> Und ein Poet muss dergestalt, sowohl als
> ein Mahler, Bildschnitzer u.s.w. eine
> starcke Einbildungs-Krafft, viel Scharf-
> sinnigkeit und einen grossen Witz schon
> von Natur besitzen, wenn er den Nahmen
> eines Dichters mit Recht führen will
> (VCD, pp. 86-87).

Other necessary attributes of the poet are "einen hohen Grad
der Aufmercksamkeit" (VCD, p. 88).

> So wird denn ein Poet, der auch die unsichtbaren
> Gedancken und Neigungen menschlicher Gemüther
> nachzuahmen hat, sich nicht ohne eine weitläuftige
> Gelehrsamkeit behelfen können (VCD, p. 88).

It is in this harmony between all of the constituents of the
creative faculty of the artist which generates the power to
move the beholder of art[6]. And in this conception of the
artist there is an affinity with Gottsched's understanding of
the ancient poets who he calls the first "Weltweisen". The

peculiar attraction of these ancient poets is their ability to combine "viel Witz", a "lebhaffte Einbildungs-Krafft", "Verstand" and "hohe Weisheit" (VCD, p. 75). Again, the ancients are held up as models for modern poets.

It is important to note then that the proper function of the creative imagination for Gottsched is quite similar to Bodmer's formulation of the same.

> Die Einbildungs-Krafft nehmlich bringet
> bey den gegenwärtigen Empfindungen sehr
> leicht wiederum die Begriffe hervor, die
> wir sonst schon gehabt; wenn sie nur die
> geringste Aehnlichkeit damit haben (VCD, p. 86).

The imagination, then, is primarily a reproductive faculty, which recalls to the attention of the beholder those sensations which were experienced upon first contact with an object. Its creativity, however, lies in its contribution to the art of expression. Like Bodmer, Gottsched emphasizes the importance of figures of speech which constitute "eine Sprache der Affecten", and "einen Ausdruck starcker Gemüths-Bewegungen", by which means one "gleichfalls die innere Gemüths-Beschaffenheit von aussen abnehmen kan" (VCD, p. 259).

> Die gantze Stärcke einer Rede zeiget sich darinn,
> weil sie ein gewisses Feuer in sich enthalten,
> welches auch den Lesern oder Zuhörern, durch eine
> geheime Kunst, Füncken ins Hertz wirft, und sie
> gleichergestalt entzündet (VCD, p. 259).

B. The Philosophical Account of the
Einbildungskraft in the Weltweisheit

In the chapter, "Von der Einbildungskraft und dem Gedächtnisse", of the Erste Gründe der gesammten Weltweisheit

(1733), the creative imagination is understood as producing less clear and distinct impressions than sensual perceptions. Nonetheless, when divorced from sensation, this faculty gains an equivalent strength (W, I, p. 483). Gottsched then postulates a rule, similar to Bodmer's understanding, that this faculty is primarily responsible for the reproduction of objects and sensations long forgotten:

> Vermöge derselben muss uns bey einem ähnlichen
> Dinge das andere, und bey einem Theile einer
> vormaligen Empfindung, die ganze damalige
> Vorstellung einfallen (EGW, I, p. 484).

With respect to memory, Gottsched insists that it is actually the imagination which ignites our memory, for this is "eine Kraft" which awakens "vergangene Gedancken" (EGW, I, p. 486).

Like Bodmer, Gottsched maintains that the creative imagination is responsible for the creation of other ideas never before imagined. Yet, it is limited in its power, for it combines something new with something already known: "es mag um diese Verbindung einen zulänglichen Grund haben, oder nicht" (EGW, I, p. 484). As we shall discover, this definition qualifies as an early formulation of what Baumgarten was to define as "das Wunderbare" in poesy.

Mere dreaming or phantasizing, however, in that it lacks sufficient cause ("ein zureichender Grund") is sharply divorced from the workings of the imagination (EGW, I, p. 484). Those "ungeschickte" artists who incorporate such ramblings on into their work are said to bring about nothing more than "laute

Grotesken, Quodlibete und Misgeburten" (<u>EGW</u>, I, pp. 484-485).

"Geschickte" artists, however, rely on "eine vernünftige
Dicht- und Erfindungskraft" and base their art on nature in
accordance with the "Vorschrift menschlicher Leidenschaften"
and the "Vorbilde der wirklich vorhandenen Dinge, darinn alles
zu leben scheint" (<u>EGW</u>, I, p. 485).

Gottsched, then, perceives of the <u>Einbildungskraft</u> as
bringing forth primarily "lauter Begriffe von vormaligen
Empfindungen" (<u>EGW</u>, I, p. 533). Yet, there is an important
differentiation to be noted:

> ...dass sich die Seele in ihren Einbildungen
> den vergangenen Zustand der Welt vorstellet;
> oder auch wohl den künftigen, und bloss
> möglichen, in so weit er aus Zusammensetzung
> alter Theile erwachsen kann. Doch, da die
> Kraft der Seele eingeschränkt ist, so bringet
> sie auch von ihren vormaligen Empfindungen
> nur diejenigen hervor, die mit dem Gegenwärtigen
> etwas gemein haben: wie die Regel der
> Einbildungskraft solches zeiget (<u>EGW</u>, I, p. 533).

In summarizing our findings, we now understand that the
uniqueness of the creative imagination for Gottsched consists
in its ability to create possible occurrences by combining unknown images with known events. Although the imagination was
ascribed an equal position with <u>Witz</u> and <u>Scharfsinnigkeit</u> in
the creative production of works of art in the <u>Critische</u>
<u>Dichtkunst</u>, this faculty is given a new freedom some three
years later in Gottsched's philosophical treatise. The
imagination is no longer limited to the reproduction of forgotten sensations, as H. P. Herrmann maintains[7], but given a
new vitality in its ability to create images never before

perceived by the beholder of art. In this way, Gottsched's thoughts contributed substantially to the further development of the idea of the creative spontaneity of the imagination and its central role in the creation of works of art.

III. Breitinger and the Abstractionem Imaginationis

It was up to Breitinger to place the imagination at the very center of the creative process. The Abstractionem Imaginationis ("die Abgezogenheit der Einbildung"), which creates "durch eine neue Zusammenordnung der Bilder aus der materialischen so wohl als aus der moralischen Welt so wunderbare Vorstellungen" (CD, I, p. 286), draws upon that "unerschöpfliche Schatzkammer" of "mögliche Welten" (CD, I, p. 264) in the creation of works of art. Creative imagination, then, constitutes the very essence of poetic truth ("das poetische Wahre"):

> Das Wahre des Verstandes gehöret für die
> Weltweisheit, hingegen eignet der Poet
> sich das Wahre der Einbildungskraft zu
> (CD, I, pp. 138-139).

Poetic truth is created in the "Uebereinstimmung des Gemähldes mit möglichen Urbildern" (CD, I, p. 52). So it is the creative imagination of the artist which effects the transformation of the real into the possible and which gives rise to the new and the marvelous.

Although poetic truth is "der Grundstein des Ergetzens" (CD, I, p. 67), "das Neue" is perceived as "eine Mutter des Wunderbaren, und hiemit eine Quelle des Ergetzens" (CD, I,

p. 110). Breitinger's formulations concerning the new and
the marvelous proceed from the basic assumption that not everything which is natural and true possesses the power to move us,
"sondern dass diese Gabe alleine dem Neuen, Ungewohnten,
Seltzamen, und Ausserordentlichen zukomme" (CD, I, p. 110).

> Je neuer demnach, je unbekannter, je unerwarteter
> eine Vorstellung ist, desto grösser muss auch das
> Ergetzen seyn (CD, I, p. 112).

"Das Wunderbare"[8] is "die äusserste Staffel des Neuen"
(CD, I, p. 130). The special function of the marvelous consists in its effect upon the beholder:

> ...es verkleidet die Wahrheit in eine ganz
> fremde, aber durchsichtige Maske, sie den
> achtlosen Menschen desto beliebter und
> angenehmer zu machen (CD, I, p. 130).

Whereas with "das Neue", truth, understood as appearance or
poetic truth, dominates falsity ("das Falsche"), in the presentation of "das Wunderbare", falsity is said to reign over
truth. What Breitinger means here is that our first perception of the marvelous, which has the appearance of contradict-
ing all that we know to be true in actual life, radiates a
semblance of falsity to our understanding.

When Breitinger ascribes to the creative imagination a
certain logic[9], this is meant simply as an analogue to the
logic of the understanding. Similar to the logic of the
understanding, this "Logik der Phantasie" is responsible for
maintaining an orderly, non-contradictory progression of
images. Unlike the understanding, however, the imagination is
not at all concerned with the true essence or ground of things,

but remains content with outward appearances. It is with
the "Gestalt und Beschaffenheit der Sachen" and with their
depiction "in so geschickten und lebhaften Bildern" that
poetry is most deeply concerned (CAG, p. 7), and wherein probability takes the place of truth (CAG, p. 8).

Although "das Wunderbare" is nothing more and nothing less
than "ein vermummetes Wahrscheinliches" (CD, I, p. 132), the
decisive point is that such marvelous occurrences must correspond not with what we know, but with what we believe to be
possible (CD, I, p. 132). As in Bodmer's essay (1727), this
equating of "probable" with "believable" has significant con-
sequences. For in so doing, Breitinger further expands the
limits of probability, by having the imagination of the beholder be the final judge of what is probable. So that what
is probable to the imagination may not always be accessible to
the understanding.

> Da nun die Poesie eine Nachahmung der Schöpfung
> und der Natur nicht nur in dem Würcklichen,
> sondern auch in dem Möglichen ist, so muss
> ihre Dichtung, die eine Art der Schöpfung ist,
> ihre Wahrscheinlichkeit entweder in der
> Uebereinstimmung mit den gegenwärtiger Zeit
> eingeführten Gesetzen und dem Laufe der Natur
> gründen, oder in den Kräften der Natur, welche
> sie bey andern Absichten nach unsern Begriffen
> hätte ausüben können. Beydemahl bestehet die
> Wahrscheinlichkeit darinn, dass die Umstände
> mit der Absicht übereinstimmen, dass sie selber
> in einander gegründet seyn, und sich zwischen
> denselben kein Widerspruch erzeige (CD, I, pp.
> 136-137).

Quite emphatic is Breitinger's insistence that, in the invention ("Erdichtung") of new worlds, new laws are created and

that what is required is only "dass das Wunderbare nicht

ungläublich werde und allen Schein der Wahrheit verliehre"

(CD, I, p. 137).

> Er [der Poet] muss darum, seine Freyheit
> zu erdichten, wenigst nach dem Wahne des
> grösten Haufens der Menschen einschräncken,
> und nichts vorbringen, als was er weiss,
> dass es schon einigermaassen in demselben
> gegründet ist (CD, I, p. 137).

What is probable, then, is determined solely by the imagination

of the beholder of art.

Although Alexander Baumgarten in his Meditationes of 1735

had already allowed for the incorporation of the marvelous into

poetic works of art, his definition of the same is restrictive.

In Paragraph 48, we read:

> Wenn also Wunderbares vorgestellt werden soll,
> so muss doch etwas bei seiner Vorstellung
> verworren wiedererkannt werden können; d.h.:
> im Wunderbaren selbst geschickt Bekanntes mit
> Unbekanntem zu mischen, ist äusserst poetisch[10]

Where Breitinger differs from Baumgarten is on the point of the

recognition of something already known or at least familiar to

our consciousness in the comprehension of the marvelous.

Breitinger's concept of the marvelous includes nothing of this

and grants to the imagination the free invention of events

never before beheld by the onlooker.

Whereas Bodmer had understood the imagination more in

terms of Addison's concept of the "secondary pleasures of the

imagination", i.e. as those objects which had at one time

entered our eyes and were then recalled to our consciousness,

Breitinger concentrates on the power of the artist to generate

new and marvelous occurrences never before perceived. In so
doing, Breitinger ascribed to the creative imagination an
originality, power and autonomy hitherto unknown.

> Denn was ist Dichten anders, als sich in
> der Phantasie neue Begriffe und Vorstellungen
> formieren, deren Originale nicht in der
> gegenwärtigen Welt der würcklichen Dinge,
> sondern in irgend einem andern möglichen
> Welt-Gebäude zu suchen sind. Ein jedes
> wohlerfundenes Gedicht ist darum nicht
> anderst anzusehen, als eine Historie aus
> einer andern möglichen Welt: Und in der
> Absicht kömmt auch dem Dichter alleine
> der Nahme Ποιητοῦ , eines Schöpfers, zu, weil
> er nicht alleine durch seine Kunst unsichtbaren
> Dingen sichtbare Leiber mittheilet, sondern
> auch die Dinge, die nicht für die Sinnen sind,
> gleichsam erschaffet, das ist, aus dem Stande
> der Möglichkeit in den Stand der Würcklichkeit
> hinüberbringet, und ihnen also den Schein und
> den Nahmen des Würcklichen mittheilet" (CD, I,
> pp. 59-60).[11]

With this insight, Breitinger again reveals the true nature of
the literary artist. In that the poet creatively imitates the
art of the Creator, he becomes, as Shaftesbury was the first
to proclaim, a "second Maker; a just Prometheus, under Jove".[12]

More extensive insights into Breitinger's position are won
from his discussion of what he understands as constituting one
of the sources of "das Wunderbare", namely, "ein angenehme [r]
Betrug der Begierden oder Gemüthes-Neigungen" (CD, I, p. 307).

Speaking of the power of the imagination in general,
Bodmer notes that when one is carried away by emotion, a
pleasant confusion predominates and reason and understanding
are unable to win an audience. For when sparked by passion the
"erhitzte Phantasie...ist von dem Verstande und den Sinnen
gantz abgezogen, und in sich selbst hinein gekehrt" (CD, I,

p. 308). When ignited by enthusiasm, the imagination follows
its own impulses, irrespective of the demands of the senses or
of the understanding (Bodmer!). This is why Breitinger
stresses time and again that it is not the poet's function to
describe natural objects in their actual proportion, but "wie
sie einem aufmercksamen Zuschauer wahrscheinlich vorkommen"
(CD, I, p. 303; see also, CD, I, pp. 287, 289, 309-310). For
it is the poet's duty to hold his audience "in einer beständi-
gen Unruhe" (CD, I, p. 309). In that the function of art,
then, involves the transmission of "den Schein eines Lebens und
einer Bewegung" (CD, I, p. 303), the poet is expected to create,
through this "Betrug der Affecte", the images which are both
"wunderbar" and "hertzrührend" (CD, I, p. 310).

> Kurtz, die Phantasie, die durch die Leidenschaften
> erhitzet ihren Träumen nachhängt, sieht die Dinge,
> die vor Augen liegen, entweder gar nicht, oder in
> einer gantz andern Grösse, Figur und Gestalt, als
> sie haben; Hingegen bildet sie sich ein, dass sie
> dasjenige würcklich sehe, was sie wünschet oder
> fürchtet, wenn es schon nicht vorhanden ist, und
> daher entstehen die wunderbaren und seltsamen
> Vorstellungen der Phantasie, die poetischen
> Entzückungen, Gesichter, Weissagungen, Träume
> welche vornehmlich in der Ode herrschen, und von
> dem poetischen Enthusiasmo oder der Begeisterung
> herrühren (CD, I, p. 309).

It is not simply by accident that Breitinger should refer
specifically to the ode in this context. For the ode is the
best literary form for the exhaltation of God and the wonders
of His Creation. Indeed, it is as if Breitinger is suggesting
that the literary artist, as an imitator of the art of God,
most creatively expresses his nearness to God through the

medium of the ode. Considering this glorification of the ode

and the creation of marvelous and heart-stirring events, it is

little wonder that Klopstock would soon become the German

Pindar in the eyes of the Zürich critics[13].

Like Bodmer (VEK), Breitinger perceives the power of the

imagination to move as rivaling that of sensation:

> ...die aufgebrachte, und durch eine strenge
> anhaltende Leidenschaft erhitzte Phantasie
> wird öfters so sehr verzücket, dass sie ihre
> lebhaften Einbildungen von den Empfindungen
> gegenwärtiger Dinge nicht wohl unterscheiden kan;...
> (CD, I, p. 322).

Baumgarten, as well, had made the arousal of sensation by way of

such "Einbildungen" the very key to poetry. In what seems to be

an indirect attack on the poets of the Second Silesian School,

Baumgarten, in the 29th Paragraph of his Meditationes, asserts:

> Da Empfindungen durch Erregung von Affekten
> bestimmt werden, ist ein Gedicht, das Affekte
> erregt, vollkommener als eines voll toter
> Einbildungen,...Es ist also poetischer,
> Affekte zu erregen, als Phantasien zu erzeugen
> (Med, p. 115).

Or, as Bodmer was to note later in the Neue Critische Briefe

(1749):

> Nun ist es eigentlich das Geschäft der Poesie,
> die Sachen die über die Sinnen und die
> Einbildung hinweg sind, zu derselben herunter
> zu ziehen, indem sie selbige sinnlich und
> empfindlich machet (NCB, p. 26).

That poetry was able to move and affect the beholder was

directly attributable to the creative imagination. This is one

of the points of commonality among all the early Aufklärer.

For Breitinger, the imagination produces such "Phantasie-

Bilder" (fear, jealously, and love, for instance) which serve
as "ein namhaftes Mittel den Geist zu erheben" (CD, I, p. 323).
Those "Einbildungen" of speech which are based on the expression
of particular emotions likewise constitute "ein vornehmer
Kunstgriff, die Rede zu erheben", and make poetry "prächtig und
nachdrücklich-lebhaft" (CD, I, p. 323). Both means serve the
purpose of presenting to the imagination of the beholder events
which appear to be taking place before our very eyes (CD, I,
pp. 322, 323, etc.). In this way, poetic images are able to
move us as powerfully as actual experience.

For concrete examples of this peculiar "Schwung der
Einbildungs-Kraft", Breitinger cites excerpts from two of
Johann Ulrich König's poems and from one of Gottsched's
contributions. For purposes of comparison we cite the strophe
by Gottsched:

> Wenn wird das menschliche Geschlecht
> Doch endlich seiner Wuth vergessen,
> Und sich nach Billigkeit und Recht,
> Nicht nach der blinden Macht gestählter Fäuste messen!
> Zurück, ihr Furien, zurück!
> Verbergt nur euren finstern Blick
> In des Avernus Pfuhl, und räumt den Kreis der Erden:
> Irenens Gottheit zeigt sich schon,
> Sie pflanzt sich unter uns den Thron,
> Und gantz Europa soll ein Friedens-Tempel werden

In comparison with Gottsched's poem which J.E. Schlegel
cites as an example of extensive clarity (p. 47, Chapter I,)
the present poem is far more moving. And this is primarily because the earlier poem is exemplary of a study in imitation,
where the latter is an expression of enthusiasm in the form of
yearning. The imagination is "erhitzt". This is particularly

evident in Line 5. This line is the shortest in meter (3 beats), the most imaginative, and carries the most impact. It expresses a desperate cry for the Furies (the powers of Europe) to relent in their vengefulness. Almost as quickly as the cry has been uttered, however, there follows that great vision of a golden age, when Europe stands as the model of peace. It is a far more moving expression than the previous poem and yet it shares with the former that vividness of imagery and clarity of description which was demanded of the poetry of this time. What has been added is a greater measure of creative imagination and poetic enthusiasm.

In reference to König's poems, Breitinger reveals one of the criteria of good poetry. Pointing to the heroic ode of 1725, written on the occasion of the birth of a Saxon princess (one of the most revered poems of the time), Breitinger favors the "künstliche Verwirrung" and the "durch den Verstand geleitete Entzückung" (CD, I, p. 325). For Breitinger, the poem is a model ode which appeals both to the senses and to the understanding.

> ...
> Seht wie die Laster flieh'n vor ihrem Angesicht!
> O! Wer erkennt sie wohl im ersten Anblick nicht!
> Josepha kommt in diesem Reihen
> Den ersten Ausgang Gott zu weihen.

Breitinger's praise stems primarily from the creative vision of the princess ascending the temple. It is the awe ("Verwunderung") of beholding the majesty of the procession, i.e. König's "prophetische Entzückung" (CD, I, p. 327) that arouses

Breitinger's admiration.

The critic's admiration for "prophetische Entzückung",
however, must not be confused with "göttliche Begeisterung".
This is where Breitinger and the ancients, not to mention
those moderns who believed in divine inspiration, part company.

> Kurz, das Geheimniss, so darunter verborgen
> liegt, will nichts weiters sagen, als eine
> Hi [t] ze der Einbildungskraft...(CD, I, p. 331).

The "poetische Begeisterung" which seems to inform that poetry
which speaks of the activities of the gods and incorporates
the "Raserey der Priester" is nothing more than "eine künstliche·
Nachahmung der Reden und Aussprüche solcher Personen, die sich
himmlischer Erscheinungen und prophetischen Eingebungen
rühmen" (CD, I, p. 331). Skillful imitation, poetic enthusiasm
and creative imagination explain the semblance of divine inspiration.

> Also siehet man, dass die Begeisterung zur
> Kunst des Poeten gehöret, und das Ansehen
> von etwas göttlichem dadurch erworben, weil
> sie die göttlichen Begeisterungen geschickt
> nachzuahmen gewusst hat (CD, I, p. 331)

On the subject of the imitation of priestly "Raserey", for
example, we win some insights into the working of the creative
process. The chief problem in this instance is to make an
emotion which is aroused as a result of the subject matter moving ("rege"). This is accomplished, first, by choosing an
aspect of the subject which has never before been perceived by
the beholder. Next, the poet must be careful to select only
those "Bilder der Phantasie" which are useful to his purpose.

Since each emotion can be aroused by the introduction of a particular object known to cause that emotion, so also will each subject ignite our imagination and, consequently, set us in "Raserey".

> Derowegen müssen die Poeten Fleiss anwenden,
> dass sie mittelst der Kunst einen Affect in
> Absicht auf die Materie, von der sie handeln
> wollen, bey sich rege machen" (CD I, pp. 332-333).

The soul will thus command the creative imagination to survey the object and then, when sparked by emotion, i.e. set into motion, will create those "neue und wunderbare Bilder" which are necessary for the creation of "ein ungewöhnliches Licht und Leben" (CD, I, p. 333) which is art.

Nevertheless, the poet must never transcend that probability which is based on a "Betrug der Affecte" and even "der erhi[t]zteste Poet" must have "ein gesundes Urtheil" (CD, I, p. 331). For Breitinger is careful to note "dass man das rechte Maass nicht übersteige" (CD, I, p. 333).

Creative imagination and imitation, poetic enthusiasm and sensible judgment, emotion and reason--these are the poles between which the mind of the poet vacillates.

In retrospect, we have established that Bodmer (1727), Gottsched (1730), and Baumgarten (1735) were basically united in their perception of the creative imagination. Drawing upon the definition of the imagination as found in Suida's lexicon, Baumgarten asserts:

> Was sind also Einbildungen anders, als
> neu gebildete (wiedererzeugte) Bilder

(Vorstellungen) von sinnlichen Dingen,
die von den Sinnen aufgenommen wurden,
was schon·mit dem Begriff sinnliche Dinge
ausgedrückt wird? (Med., P. 28, p. 115).

The primary concern of the Einbildungskraft, then, is with the

"Reproduktion von Sinneswahrnehmungen" (Med., p. 115), an

understanding which is reflected again in Adelung's

Grammatisch-Kritisches Wörterbuch of 1774. Here, the creative

imagination is defined as:

> ...das Vermögen der Seele, sich ein Bild,
> oder eine Vorstellung von einer abwesenden [!]
> Sache zu machen, in der weitesten Bedeutung
> des Zeitwortes, einbilden. Eine starke
> Einbildungskraft, welche sich das abwesende
> klar und deutlich vorstellen kann (I, p. 1551).

In the Fifth Chapter of his Metaphysics, Vernünftige

Gedanken von Gott, der Welt und der Seele des Menschen (1720),

entitled "Von dem Wesen der Seele und des Geistes überhaupt",

Christian Wolff perceived of the imagination as a solely re-

productive faculty:

> Die Einbildungskraft bringet nichts hervor,
> als was wir vor diesem empfunden oder gedacht,
> und also sind die Einbildungen nichts anders
> als Vorstellungen von vergangenem Zustande
> der Welt[14].

Most critics of the early Aufklärung have endeavored to explain

both Bodmer's and Gottsched's concepts of the imagination

solely in terms of Wolff's definition. Although Wolff's ex-

planation serves as the point of departure for Bodmer, Gottsched,

and even Baumgarten, all three, albeit gradually, begin to ex-

pand the limits of the creative imagination.

By insisting that the imagination must operate alone, as

divorced from sensation, in order that "Einbildungen" may assume the same status, i.e. generate an equivalent effect as that of "Empfindungen", Bodmer, already in 1727, attributed to the imagination a certain freedom of creation. This freedom of expression is made explicit in Gottsched's Weltweisheit of 1733, where Gottsched expressly states that the imagination creates ideas which have never before been perceived[15]. The emphasis, then, has shifted from the reproductive function of the imagination to its creative potential. The imagination does not simply recall events of the past, but generates future or even merely possible ("künftige und bloss mögliche") occurrences. Baumgarten's concept of "das Wunderbare" further expanded the limits of imagination by ascribing to the imagination the power of combining familiar with unknown occurrences. In this way, all three critics transcended the bounds which Wolff had placed on the imagination.

Christian Wolff's formulation is not representative, then, of a common idea concerning the imagination at the time of the early German Aufklärung, but simply serves as the point of departure for the early Aufklärer.

For Bodmer of 1740, however, as for Breitinger, the creative imagination has been freed of its reproductive function and has been attributed far greater freedom in the creation of imaginative events. The poet, like a second creator, creates his works of art through the auspices of a seemingly divinely-inspired imagination.

> Der Poet, dessen Werck ist die Kräfte der Natur
> in der Ueberbringung des Möglichen in den Stand
> der Würcklichkeit, nachzuahmeń, hat also das
> Nichts, das vor der Schöpfung war, schon als
> etwas vorgestellet, und damit die Schöpfung
> vor der Schöpfung vorausgeholet (CAW, p. 165).

This creation of new and marvelous images now becomes the

essence of "poetische Erschaffung" (CAW, p. 166) for Bodmer,

and the proper function of the creative imagination, "weil der

Poet...da kein Muster vor sich habe, dem er folgen könte,

sondern mit seiner eignen Einbildungs-Kraft arbeiten müsste..."

(CAW, p. 167). For:

> ...es ist keine grössere Kühnheit des Nichts
> als etwas vorzustellen, als es ist, das Mögliche
> vor würcklich vorzubilden; denn das Mögliche
> ist eben sowohl noch nichts, und was ist, was
> etwas ist, war zuvor nur möglich (CAW, p. 164).

In the main assessments of the power of the creative

imagination at the time of the early Aufklärung, there is

commonality in that the creative imagination is afforded all

freedom short of improbability. As we have seen, however,

there is divergence among these early critics in their formula-

tions concerning the specific nature of this central poetic

faculty. And at the same time, there is an unmistakable ex-

pansion of the limits of probability in order to facilitate

such phenomena as the new and the marvelous.

We therefore conclude that, by 1740, the Einbildungskraft

had become the essence of artistic creativity. Its primary

function was now the creation of new and marvelous images which

were capable of overwhelming the beholder. The imagination was

perceived as a highly creative faculty which, like that of God,

was capable of creating new and possible worlds out of nothing. The mind of the artist was now attributed a power and
significance hitherto unknown in Germany's intellectual history.

CHAPTER III

ON TASTE, BEAUTY AND THE SUBLIME

> But there is nothing that makes
> its way more directly to the Soul
> than Beauty, which immediately
> diffuses a secret satisfaction and
> Complacency through the Imagina-
> tion, and gives a Finishing to
> anything that is Great or Un-
> common (Joseph Addison).

The transition from the Baroque to the Aufklärung in
Germany is marked by the heated polemics and generally negative
criticism on the part of the early Aufklärer against the Second
Silesian School poets. As Johann Ulrich König (1688-1744)
notes[1], Christian Wernicke (1661-1725) was the first to
publicly renounce the Lohensteinian style in the preface to his
own collection of poems, entitled, Poetischer Versuch in einem
Helden- und Schäfer-Gedichte durch Uberschrifften (1704).
And, as Gottsched informs us, Andreas Gryphius was the first to
suggest that there was something amiss with the style of the
Second Silesian School poets in his Poetische Wälder (VCD, p.
228).

In his short "Einleitung zu der allgemeinen Geschichte
des guten Geschmacks", which begins the Untersuchung von dem
Guten Geschmack In der Dicht- und Rede-Kunst of 1727, Johann
Ulrich König cites as the true cause of the corruption of
taste in Germany the infiltration of the Marino School style

into the poetry of the Second Silesian School poets.

> Kurz: Die Lohensteinische Schule bekam auch
> bey uns die Oberhand über den guten Geschmack,
> und verleitete fast ganz Teutschland so wohl,
> als die meisten seiner Lands-Leute (UGG, p. 236).

"Schwülstige Metaphoren, falsche Gedancken, gezwungene Künsteleyen, lächerliche Spitzfindigkeiten"--this was the result of the poison ("Gifft") of Marinism (Giambattista Marino (1569-1625)).

Near the end of the 17th Century, however, König discerns a turn for the good and a deeper appreciation of what he understands as constituting good Taste in the work of Herr von Besser and the Freyherr von Canitz. These "trefliche Köpfe", by grounding their works solidly upon Nature and the ancients, are credited with restoring good Taste to Germany (UGG, p. 238). Problematical, however, as König notes, was that the general reading public still preferred the bombast ("Schwulst") of the Lohenstein School (UGG, p. 239).

The early Aufklärer, then, endeavored to restore to Germany's literary consciousness the good Taste which was said to have flourished in the writings of Martin Opitz. Because of this contrasting of the Second Silesian School poets with Opitz the early German Aufklärung must be viewed both as a reaction against and a continuation of the Baroque tradition.

That this sometimes polemical, sometimes justifiable critical assault was uppermost in the minds of the Aufklärer is obvious as late as 1760, in Gottsched's Handlexikon. After differentiating between the pomposity of the early

Benjamin Neukirch (1665-1729) and the "völlige Bekehrung"
(expressed in Pietistic terms) of the post-1700 Neukirch,
Gottsched cites what he believes to be a representatively distasteful poem and concludes:

> Solche Beyspiele müssen uns behutsam machen,
> dass wir uns weder durch den lohensteinischen,
> noch marinischen oder miltonischen [!] Schwulst
> dahin reissen, oder anstecken lassen; sondern
> der gefunden opitzischen Bahn folgen mögen
> (Handlexikon, p. 1171).

This attack on the Lohenstein School, however, has far
deeper roots than in the mere preference for the poetry of
Besser and Canitz over that of Lohenstein and Hofmannswaldau.
The deep concern for the purification of the German language,
as exemplified in Gottsched's attempts and successes in
developing a common orthography on the basis of a single
dialect (Meissen), was first expressed by Leibniz in his Von
deutscher Sprachpflege[2]. Here, the philosopher-mathematician
exhorts the German people to purify their language with the aid
of the understanding. Language, perceived as "ein Spiegel des
Verstandes" (VdS, Paragraph 1, p. 25), must be purified of its
great dependency upon foreign borrowings and be refined
through "Verstandesübung". Words are defined as symbols of
thought (VdS, P. 5, p. 26) and as such contribute to the
orderliness, i.e. clarity of expression, of a language. This
linguistic purification is said to be useful not only for
scholars and poets, but for the common man who engages in
everyday intercourse and business transactions (VdS, P. 9,
p. 27). Linguistic purity, then, is directly related to the

development of a sense of national identity, based on good
Taste.

Leibniz is careful to note, however, that extremism in
such an endeavor, i.e., of viewing every use of a word of
foreign origin as a cardinal sin ("eine Todsünde"), leads only
to "Scheinreinigkeit" (VdS, P. 16, p. 29). Leibniz's
encouragement of the work of the Fruchtbringende Gesellschaft,
then, would not be extended to those extremists in its midst
who transcended reasonableness in order to create a sometimes
laughable "Germanic" word to replace a perfectly acceptable
and commonly used derivative.

"Reichtum", "Reinigkeit" and "Glanz" were required in
the development of a national language. That the German
language soon began to develop a national integrity among the
languages of Europe is directly attributable to the work of
Johann Christoph Gottsched[3].

Just as Leibniz was concerned with the purification of
the German language "von dem überflüssigen fremden Mischmasch"
(VdS, P. 73, p. 44), so also was it the concern of literary
critics and poetologists to purify poetry of its excessive
ornamentation and meaningless pomposity.

In his essay, "Von der Schönheit der Deutschen Sprache in
Absicht auf ihre Bedeutung", the second contribution to the
Beyträge Zur Kritischen Historie Der Deutschen Sprache, Poesie,
und Beredsamkeit (1732ff.), Gottsched defines the beauty of a
language in terms of its perfection. Every word of the German

language is beautiful when there is perfect harmony of all the various parts of speech (BKH, I, p. 57). Clarity of expression implies perfection, for it is the purpose of language to communicate thoughts through words (BKH, I, p. 56). So that the further one digresses from clarity, the further one distances oneself from beautiful expression (BKH, I, p. 58). "Die Pflicht eines Deutschen" is to guard against a lack of clarity and definition in the maintenance of "die Ehre seiner Sprache" (BKH, I, p. 58). Again, the preservation of linguistic purity instills a sense of national identity.

With respect to language, there are two kinds of beauty in Gottsched's estimation. "Einfache" beauty applies to lexical entries and semantics, while "zusammengesetzte" beauty refers to syntactic constructions. One must guard "dass man die Bedeutung und den Verstand der Worte nicht zu tief versteckt" (BKH, I, p. 62) and figures of speech ("Redensarten") must not be overstated ("übersteigend"), as, for example, in the work of Lohenstein, who Gottsched accuses of having succumbed to the "Schwulst der Italienischen Sprache" (BKH, I, p. 63).

Gottsched's investigation of language, therefore, is not only important from a linguistic standpoint, but especially because of its ramifications for the history of poetics and aesthetics. The Second Silesian School poets lack good Taste because of their bombastic excesses and exaggeration. Their language transcends the bounds of clarity of expression, logic and plausibility and therefore operates in opposition to the ideal of a beautiful language[4].

This is the true meaning of the cultivation of good Taste and the idealisation of the Good, the True and the Beautiful which typify the writings of essentially all early Aufklärer.

In this chapter we attempt to offer a new account of the concept of Taste and the ideas of the beautiful and the sublime during the time of the early German Aufklärung, i.e. prior to the appearance of that first scientific and systematic treatment of the beautiful in Germany, Alexander Baumgarten's Aesthetica (1750).

I. Bodmer and Die Discourse der Mahlern

Die Discourse der Mahlern (1721-1723), "the first important imitation of the English weeklies in the German tongue"[5], enjoyed only two years of publication. Not only did the Zürich censorship make difficulties because of the at times questionable moral and political connotations of the Discourses[6], but the club itself (Gesellschaft der Mahlern) simply grew tired of its own deliberations[7]. Despite this early misfortune, however, Bodmer was able to have a revised and enlarged edition of the Discourses published in 1746 under a new title: Der Mahler der Sitten[8]. We will discuss these documents in a comparative manner, as we shall do for the first and subsequent editions of Gottsched's Versuch einer Critischen Dichtkunst.

Our primary concern here is with Bodmer's concept of

beauty which we find elaborated in Part II, the Twentieth
Discourse.

Since Bodmer did not take up the study of English until
sometime after the appearance of The Spectator, he was obliged
to refer to the incomplete French translation of Addison's
journal (200 of the 555 entries were included) which appeared
in Amsterdam (in six editions!, [1] 1714; [6] 1744), bearing the
title, Le Spectateur ou le Socrate moderne, ou l'on voit un
portrait naif des moeurs de ce siècle[9].

As Benedetto Croce not unreasonably points out,
"Eighteenth-Century Aesthetics are dominated by the enquiry
into and the discussion of the theory of taste"[10]. Croce's
general observation that "practically all the treatises on
taste in the 18th Century in fact end up with a theory of the
beautiful, of natural and arbitrary beauty, intellectual and
moral, visual and audible beauty, beauty of bodies and spirits
and deity, and so on"[11], is certainly true of the work of
Bodmer, König and Gottsched, in particular.

In a fictitious letter addressed to the Mahler of the
Discourses, Bodmer maintains that taste and beauty are, in
fact, relative terms.

> Der Geschmack aller dieser Völkern ist
> unseren Europeern ihrem so gerad entgegen,
> dass man bey uns die Hässlichkeit mahlet,
> wie sie die Schönheit mahlen, indessen
> haben die unsere keinen Grunde ihre Meinung
> zurechtfertigen, der nicht auch den andern
> diene, um die ihre zu beweisen (DM, Part II,
> XX. Disc., p. 157).

It is Bodmer's contention that this relativity of judgment

is to be verified not only on the basis of the dissimilarity
of opinions cross-culturally, but also "wenn ihr die Begriffe,
die Menschen von der gleichen Nation dissfalls haben, gegen
einander haltet" (DM, Part II, XX. Disc., p. 157). Beauty,
then, for Bodmer, is, as for Alexander Pope, simply in the eye
of the beholder. Beauty is by nature subjective, i.e. dependent upon the perceiver's sense of judgment. And this is so,
because taste is relative.

Bodmer's statement in Der Mahler der Sitten is essentially
the same.

> Der Geschmack aller dieser Völcker von den
> Haupteigenschaften eines schönen Leibes
> streitet mit dem unsrigen gantz und gar,
> in so weit, dass man bey uns die Hässlichkeit
> schildert, wie sie die Schönheit vorstellen.
> Bey aller dieser Verschiedenheit haben unsere
> Leute keinen weitern Grund für die Behauptung
> ihrer Meinung, als ihre Empfindung, welche
> sie gern für einen sechsten Sinn ausgeben
> wollten (MS, 24. Blatt, pp. 269-270).

Even Bodmer's second argument in support of the relativity of
beauty is preserved:

> Was sie [die Empfindung] vor eine blinde
> Richterin der Schönheit sey, erhellet
> daraus, dass sie nicht nur bey verschiedenen
> Nationen, sondern auch bey verschiedenen
> Personen aus einer Nation, ja aus einer Stadt,
> ein ungleiches Urtheil ausspricht (MS, 24.
> Blatt, p. 270).

Indeed, even the form of the letter is the same as in the
Discourses. The writer of the letter is a one "Hecatissa"
("Rosenroth" in the Discourses), who the editors address as
"die Prätendentin der Schönheit".

Wolfgang Bender's statement, then, that Der Mahler der

Sitten retains little of the content and form of Die Discourse der Mahlern ("Nur noch wenig erinnert an das jugendliche
Unternehmen") is simply too strong a statement, for we find
almost identical statements on the nature of beauty in both
documents[12].

What has been brought into sharper focus on this point in
Der Mahler der Sitten, however, is that our judgment of beauty
is based solely on sensation ("die Empfindung"). It is a
subjective judgment, not an objective one. The following
passage links the two statements by Bodmer together which we
have quoted above:

> Wenn es aber auf die sinnliche Empfindung
> von dem Schönen ankommt, und man diese
> für die Richterin annimmt, so beruffen
> sich die andern, die wir Barbarn heissen,
> auf eben diesselbe; und sie spricht das
> Urtheil für sie aus, wie die Empfindung
> der andern für die andern; ein jeder hält
> sich an seine eigene, und meint, dass sie
> alleine richtig und sicher urtheile (MS,
> 24. Blatt, p. 268).

In the 412th number of The Spectator (June 23, 1712), Addison
too had expressed the thought that each of us has our own
unique idea of what constitutes beauty:

> ...we find by Experience, that there are
> several Modifications of Matter which the
> Mind, without any previous Consideration,
> pronounces at first sight Beautiful or
> Deformed. Thus we see that every different
> Species of sensible Creatures has its
> different Notions of Beauty, and that each
> of them is most affected with the Beauties
> of its own Kind (Spectator, p. 67).

Of particular interest to Bodmer is the special power of
beauty and its effect upon society. Discourse XVIII in the

Third Part (1722) of Die Discourse der Mahlern begins as
follows:

> Eine grosse Schönheit, die von einer grossen
> Tugend begleitet wird, hat einen vortrefflich
> gütigen Einfluss in die Societet (DM, Part III,
> XVIII Disc., p. 137).

"Dürer" (Bodmer?) now turns his attention to "eine vortreffliche Schönheit, die sich von der närrischen Ruhmräthigkeit
regieren läst" (DM, p. 137).

> Ich habe demnach in diesem Discours allein
> mit denen stoltzen Schönen zu thun, und man
> wird bald sehen was mich bewegt ihnen den
> Titul der Zauberinnen beyzulegen (DM, p. 138).

Beauty is here defined as "eine natürliche Zauber-
Kunst", which, "allein durch ihr Anschauen und die Minen ihres
Angesichts", can cause "die seltzamsten Wirckungen" (DM,
p. 138). However, it is the deceptively dangerous enticement
of this form of beauty, its overwhelmingly captivating power,
which is the very issue here.

Elaborating on this point, the author cites, as examples
of bewitching beauties, Venus, Circe and Helena of Greek
mythology.

> Die Schönheit hat mit einem Wort alle die
> Qualiteten, welche Homerus dem Liebes-
> Gürtel der Venus zugeschrieben hat, den
> Juno von ihr erhalten, als sie das Hertze
> des Jupiters bezaubern wollen. 'Sie
> schmirte von der Brust den Liebes-Gürtel
> loss,/ Darinn sie alle Lust und Liebes-
> Reitz beschloss,/ Begierde, Zauberey,
> Beredsamkeit, Verlangen,/ Die auch der
> klugen Hertz betrüglich können fangen
> (DM, pp. 138-139).

As for the witch, Circe, and the ravishing beauty, Helena:

Die Mythologie erzehlet Wunder von der Schönheit
und der Zauberey der Hexe Circe, die die Menschen
in Wölffe·, Schweine, Hünde, Bären und andere
unvernünfftige Thiere verwandelte. Die Wahrheit
dieser Allegorie ist, dass Circe durch die
natürliche Magie ihrer Schönheit ihre Amanten
also bezaubert, dass derselben Vernunfft ausser
die Circkel gerathen, und sie hernach mit ihnen
umgehen können, wie mit vernunfftlosen Geschöpffen.
Die Iliade des Homerus ist gleichsam das Zauber-
Buch der Schönen, und man findet darinnen die
erstaunlichen Zauber-Wercke der grossen Zauberin
Helena, die durch einen Blick gantze Armeen auf
die Wahlstatt geführt, Städte in den Brand gelegt,
und Länder verheeret hat (DM, pp. 140-141).

According to the author, the magically deceptive power of a

promiscuous beauty is discernible not only in mythology, but

within contemporary society as well.

Eine schöne Zauberin findet sich bey
allen öffentlichen Versammlungen und
den volckreichsten Platzen ein, die
Macht ihrer zauberischen Grimacen zu
versuchen (DM, pp. 139-140).

And this can be dangerous, especially for a young man.

Zu Sommers-Zeit verfügen sie sich Hauffen-
weiss nach Baden; Sie verrücken einen jungen
Menschen, dass er still stehet, und sich
unverwandt auf sie kehret, sie sind Meister
seines Geruches und seines Geschmackes...
Beware! Sie führen euch in das Paradies, und
lassen euch eine Wollust empfinden, die ihr
himmlisch nennet, sie versetzen euch von
dannen in die Hölle, und übergeben euch den
empfindlichsten Schmerzen. Ihr förchtet
euch und hoffet doch, ihr bittet und schweiget,
ihr wünschet frey zu seyn, und machet euch
zu einem Sclaven (DM, p. 140).

Although this passage may raise a smile from us today, a

deeper and certainly more significant point is in the making.

It is the powerful effect of beauty which concerns us here and

its influence on the poet.

Man muss gestehen, dass wir schöne Frauens-

> Personen haben, welche diesen berühmten
> Zauberinnen des Alterthums in der Wissenschaft
> solcher verwundersamen Künsten nichts nach-
> geben; Man betrachte nur die Effecte, welche
> solche Schwartzkünstlerinnen an unsern Poeten
> ausgeübet haben (<u>DM</u>, p. 141).

The author cites three examples here of poets who, in their poetry, testify to the alluring, but deadly power of beauty. "H. M." (Mühlpfort, according to <u>Mahler</u>, p. 424) is said to have become deathly ill from the mere kiss of one of these beauties (<u>DM</u>, pp. 141-142). Hoffmanswaldau records how he was rendered powerless by the mere glance of a Lesbian woman-- "aber Amanda, als eine neue Circe hat ihn der Freyheit und der Vernunfft gantz beraubet, und wie ein unvernünfftig Thier herumgeführt" (<u>DM</u>, p. 142). Even Erdmann Neumeister appears to have been brought to the point of drowning by means of a single kiss: "'Mein Himmelreich wird mir zur Höllen-Pein'" (<u>DM</u>, p. 143), he exclaims. Yet, worst of all is the author's allegedly personal experience of having known a man who was driven to insanity and eventual death by a beautiful temptress (<u>DM</u>, p. 143).

But what is the significance of this viewpoint? Bodmer's moral intent is quite obvious here, and very much in keeping with the "Verbesserung der Sitten", which the editors of the Discourses hoped to advance. But, most importantly, it is quite clear that Bodmer himself was quite persistent in his criticism of the "Schwulst" and "Galimathias" which German poetry had carried over from Marino and that he endeavored to replace Second Silesian School poets with Opitz, Besser and

Canitz. Although not expressly stated, Bodmer's intent here is clear. "Eine vortreffliche Schönheit", and not the mere illusion of beauty, must be the true source of poetic inspiration for artists. The "Morale dieses Discourses" is that beauty can at times conceal a distasteful and basically immoral content. Bodmer therefore makes a clear differentiation between the appearance and the reality of beauty. And his final words, although serving as a warning to all men, could easily be interpreted as advice to any author:

> ...dass sie sich niemahlen allen bey diesen
> schönen Aussenwercken der Haut, der Gliedmassen,
> und ihrer reitzenden Gebehreden aufhalten,
> sondern durch dieselben auf das Gemüthe hindurch
> dringen...Es ist ein ruhmräthiger, bosshaffter
> und ungeschliffener Geist verborgen, der...euch
> ein entsetzlich Abscheuen einjagen würde (DM,
> pp. 143-144).

Indeed, it would be impossible to paint "den schnöden Geist der darunter steckt" (DM, p. 144) any way but ugly, "als einer hässlichen Vettel, mit grauem Haupte, krummem Rücken, hägern Armen, zitterndem Gang und geflickten Schauben" (DM, p. 144).

What is most significant here, however, is that we again encounter one of the primary tasks of the early German Aufklärer: to penetrate the world of appearances with the sharpness of the critical eye!

In the First Discourse of this Third Part of Die Discourse der Mahlern, "Dürer" makes a clear distinction between the perception of beauty, on the one hand and the experience of pleasure, on the other.

> Man unterscheidet die Schönheit von der
> Annehmlichkeit; es sind schöne Leute,
> bey denen wir keine Angenehmheit finden,
> und wir sehen annehmliche Personen, die
> doch die Lineamente und Gliedmassen
> ungestaltet haben. Dieses komt daher,
> weil die Schönen lasterhafft, und die
> Garstigen tugendhafft seyn können (<u>DM</u>,
> Part III, I. Disc., p. 6).

Beauty, when coupled with or advancing the cause of virtue,
is both pleasurable and socially acceptable. Beauty, when
aligned with the demise of immorality, inflicts its beholder
with pain and contributes to the disintegration of society.
The true task of the artist, then, is clearly visible.
Through the reflection of moral beauty in the work of art, the
beholder perceives the ideal of harmony in society and is thereby moved to participate in the advancement of that ideal. This
is the deeply ethical and social function of art which was
shared by many of the early <u>Aufklärer</u>.

As revealed in the eleventh <u>Blatt</u> of <u>Der Mahler der Sitten</u>,
man and artist alike are encouraged to strive for the ideal
of the beautiful soul, whose chief attributes are a "munterer
Geist", a "scharfer Verstand", and a "liebreicher Wille" (<u>MS</u>,
I, p. 130). In much the same sense as Schiller's formulation
of the beautiful soul in <u>Naive und Sentimentalische Dichtung</u>
(1795), duty and inclination are to work harmoniously for the
common good. Beauty, then, as for the German Classics, was not
to be divorced from life.

In the realm of the aesthetic, the mere presence of beauty
in a work of art does not automatically presuppose that a
pleasurable sensation will be awakened in the beholder, anymore

(and this is the decisive point) than the perceiving of
ugliness must always arouse a painful sensation. In Discourse
II of the First Part of Die Discourse der Mahlern, we are told
that it is not only beauty which has the power of arousing
pleasure, but indeed everything (including the ugly and the
distasteful) which is well imitated.

> Hingegen ergetzet uns auch die Beschreibung
> und die Abschilderung des Lasters, der
> Bossheit, der Hässlichkeit, des Erschrecklichen,
> der Traurigen (DM, Part I, II. Disc., p. 2).

For "alles was wol nachgeahmet ist, wird uns angenehm, es seye
so grässlich und erbärmlich als es will" (DM, p. 2).

With respect to the pleasure one receives from art, then,
this can be achieved whenever there is the necessary correspondence between the artistic representation, be it beautiful
or ugly, and the natural object. Everything which is beautiful
is capable of arousing pleasure, but everything which is
pleasurable need not be beautiful. The term "schöne Künste",
then, should not be perceived as excluding the distasteful and
the ugly from the realm of the aesthetic.

In retrospect, the concept of beauty as elaborated in Die
Discourse der Mahlern reveals the prevalence of the notion of
relative or subjective beauty at the time of the early Aufklärung. Yet, in Bodmer's account, some objectivity in the
perception of beauty is admitted.

It is incumbent upon the writer to avoid the ill-effects
of deceptive beauty by drawing upon "vortreffliche Schönheit"
as the source of poetic inspiration. By piercing the world

of appearances with the sharpness of the critical eye, the literary critic must be able to differentiate between apparent and genuinely beautiful works of art. The artist, then, must contribute to the ideal of a harmoniously integrated society while the literary critic must unmask "den ungeschliffenen Geits" of deceptive beauty which arouses only "entsetzliches Abscheuen".

Although art must be morally and socially purposive, it must instruct by delighting the beholder. Indeed, the arousal of pleasure through the creative imitation of Nature is the ultimate end and the underlying principle of art. The beauty of a work or art, then, lies not in the beauty of the objects of imitation themselves, but in the beauty of the imitation. This is the decisive point of Bodmer's concept of beauty in Die Discourse der Mahlern.

In the final analysis, the perception of beauty gains objectivity by allowing time for the understanding to assess the beauty of the imitation of a work of art. And, as we shall discover, it is the uniting of sensation with understanding which characterizes aesthetic judgment for the early Aufklärer.

II. Johann Ulrich König's Untersuchung
Von dem guten Geschmack In der Dicht-
und Rede-Kunst (1727)

König's investigation of good Taste culminates in the glorification of the True, the Good, and the Beautiful, the deeply admired ideal of the ancient Greeks.

The general direction of König's thought in this essay is
toward the synthesis of external and internal, of objective and
subjective Taste. True aesthetic judgment will reflect the
mutual harmony of the sensation ("Empfindung") which one
receives upon immediate contact with an object and the somewhat delayed concept ("Begriff") of the object which one
develops upon contemplation of that object (UGG, p. 257).

Although Bodmer (VEK, pp. 16-17[13] and König (UGG, p. 239)
both defend the use of the term Geschmack to designate a refined sense of beauty, König offers a short history of the word
among the European nations. Whereas Bernardo Trevisano, in his
introduction to Muratori's work on good Taste (Introduzzione
all' opera delle Riflessioni sopra il buon gusto nelle Scienze
Arti, di Lamindo Pritanio (1717) had cited the Spanish as the
first to use the metaphor in an aesthetic sense, König suggests
that the Jews, the Greeks and the Romans, although in a less
comprehensive manner, were actually the first to use the term
in this way (UGG, pp. 240-241). The first to use the word in
the metaphorical sense in Germany was Christian Thomasius
(UGG, p. 241), who wrote the word on the black board in 1687.
It was then included in his collected works of 1721, the year
which marks the beginning of the first phase of the German
Aufklärung. After citing the important treatises on the subject at that time[14], König begins his investigation of the nature
of Taste.

Since it is "leichter zu empfinden, als zu erkennen"
(UGG, pp. 256-257), we first gain an impression of the object

before our understanding has time to render a decision concerning the aesthetic quality of that object (UGG, p. 258).
In that our soul is either attracted to or repulsed by the object, some judgment is made already upon immediate contact with
an object, without the consultation of the distinct concepts of
the understanding. And sensation, when, refined, at times has
the capacity to judge correctly in and of itself.

> Durch diese innerliche Empfindung, welche,
> nach der Meinung des Cicero, in gewisser
> Maasse allen Menschen gemein ist, entdecken
> wir, ohne Kentniss der Regeln, was an
> Kunst-Stücken gut oder schlimm ist; Ja wir
> erkennen es eher, als wir einmahl darauf
> gedacht haben, es nach den Grund-Sätzen
> der Kunst zu untersuchen (UGG, p. 263).
> [emphasis mine]

Such good Taste operates on the level of intuition without
knowledge of the rules of art and is defined as a gift of
Nature.

> Dann es ist eben der gute Geschmack, welcher
> uns durch die Empfindung dasjenige hochschätzen
> lehret, was die Vernunfft unfehlbar würde
> gebilliget haben, wann sie Zeit gehabt hätte,
> solches genugsam zu untersuchen, und durch
> Gegeneinanderhaltung der deutlichen Begriffe,
> richtig darüber zu urtheilen (UGG, p. 261).
> [emphasis mine]

Three reasons, however, prevent König from leaving good
Taste on the level of sensation alone. First, there is no
guarantee that pleasurable objects would be found acceptable
by Reason (UGG, p. 261). Secondly, there remains a lack of
certainty ("Gewissheit") of the kind distinct knowledge is
capable of providing. Finally, since not everyone possesses
this sense of accurate judgment, the understanding must be

consulted for final verification of the true beauty of a work

of art.

> Der gute Geschmack in der Dicht- und Rede-
> Kunst ist eine Fertigkeit des Verstandes,
> das wahre, gute und schöne richtig zu
> empfinden, sowohl was die Gedancken und
> die Ausdrückungen als die gantze Einrichtung
> betrifft, genau zu entscheiden: wodurch im
> Willen eine gründliche Wahl, und in der
> Ausübung eine geschickte Anwendung erfolget
> (UGG, p. 292).

Sound aesthetic judgment then proceeds both from a correct

condition of the senses (the subjective) and the critical

discernment of the understanding (the objective) (UGG, p. 258).

Essential to good Taste are not only a "gesunder Witz", a

"scharffe Urtheilungs-Krafft" and "eine feine und fertige

Empfindung", but also "Unterricht, Ubung und Untersuchung"

(UGG, pp. 263, 258). In this way, the perception of beauti-

ful things was afforded a new objectivity.

Common to all men, in König's estimation, is the capacity

of the understanding to correctly perceive the True, the

Good, and the Beautiful and to be repulsed by the False, the

Evil and the Ugly (UGG, p. 259). This is his understanding of

general Taste. But since there is no certainty without dis-

tinct knowledge, study, practice, and close investigation of

the object are required for the refinement of Taste (UGG,

p. 263). By investigation ("Untersuchung"), however, König

understands that a "fertige" ("Empfindung"), without a

"bedachtsame" ("Urtheil") "Untersuchung" leads only to

"betrügliche Anführer" (UGG, p. 276). Good Taste, then,

like true genius, does not simply come naturally, but is informed by experience and observation (UGG, pp. 268-269). While referring to that great synthesizer of thought, Leibniz, König maintains that good Taste is a product both of our natural capacity to appreciate beauty and of the practice we obtain in discerning a well-formed from an ill-formed object.

Taste per se is compared to the taste of the five senses and is understood as sensation. Good Taste, however, involves the participation of the understanding and its capacity to discern the actual from the apparent nature of things. Therefore:

> Der Geschmack schliesst allemahl eine
> Beurtheilung, aber das Urtheil nicht
> nothwendig den Geschmack in sich ein
> (UGG, p. 274).

The theological and moral sources of König's concept of Taste are revealed in his consideration of specific Taste. "Der gute geistliche Geschmack" is defined as "eine Fertigkeit der Seele", which, as a result of the use of God's Word and the means of grace, can readily distinguish between the True and the False, "und das, was wir aus Gottes Wort wissen und glauben, auch durch den Genuss zu schmecken, und lebhafft zu empfinden" (UGG, p. 277). In the moral or ethical sense, good Taste is understood as "eine fertige Gemüths-Empfindung", with the aid of which we experience either joy or disgust upon encountering an object.

With this appreciation for good Taste in all facets of life we become equipped to recognize the True, to demand the

Good, and to choose the Excellent (UGG, p. 279), the moral

advantages of which Gracian had noted in his Oraculo Manuale[15]:

> Dieser Geschmack verbessert unsre Meinungen
> und Begriffe, und leitet uns zur Selbst-
> Erkänntniss, zu der wahren Ehr-Liebe, und
> zu der Uberwindung unsrer selbst [!] (UGG, p. 279).

For "ein mit solchem guten Geschmack begabter Mensch läst sich

nicht durch seine Eigen-Liebe verführen" (UGG, p. 279).

König's formulation of good Taste, therefore, is based

upon the theological equation: "das Gute" arouses "Belustigung"

and "das Böse" "eine Verabscheuung" (UGG, p. 280). Bad Taste

is the product of greed, blind passion, and poor education

(UGG, p. 280).

The great significance of König's concept of Taste lies in

its turn from the relativism of the day to a far more objective

standard of Taste. Since, in everyday life, Taste is under-

stood merely as the power of the soul ("Gemüth") to sense and

to judge in accordance with whether an object pleases or dis-

pleases, good Taste, in order to gain objectivity, must not be

based simply on "ein Trieb des Herzens", but upon the "Wurckung

des Verstandes" (UGG, p. 285), whereby "das nützlichste,

wesentlichste und vollkommenste" (UGG, p. 286) can be ascertained.

> Er [der gute Geschmack] ist der rechte Begriff
> von allem, was in einer Wissenschaft das wahre,
> das deutliche, das erweissliche, das wahrscheinliche,
> nöthigste oder zuträglichste: In einer sinnreichen
> Kunst das schöne, meisterhaffte, edelste und feinste
> ...[ist]... (UGG, p. 286).

Consistent with König's endeavor to sharply delineate be-

tween possible kinds of Taste is his definition of the artist

in terms of Taste. We cite König's own analogy: like the
master chef who either prepares a fine meal himself or simply
tastes the delicacies of another, so the understanding expresses itself in two ways. "Der empfindende Geschmack" is
that "Fertigkeit unsrer Seele" which reveals the inadequacies
and the merits of "einer sinnreichen Schrifft" (UGG, p. 293).
"Der würckende Geschmack" is the one which is endowed with the
capacity of filling the work of art with the various attributes
of good Taste. To the artist, then, belong both the sensing and
the actively creative types of Taste for the perfection of his
art (UGG, p. 294).

That this is not merely an arbitrary differentiation is
shown, for instance, in Albrecht von Haller's (1708-1777)
letter to Bodmer of August 20, 1753. Insisting that personal
concerns had practically extinguished any "Feuer" for the
creative production of works of art (="der würckende Geschmack"),
Haller still maintains that his "Gefühle des Schönen und Wahren"
and "der Geschmack und das Vergnügen an Werken des Wi[t]zes und
des Verstandes" (i.e. der empfindende Geschmack") remain very
much alive[16].

One of König's original contributions to the history of
aesthetics is his insight that if a work of art is not well-
informed ("gut beschaffen") there can be no agreement between
the qualities which emanate from that work and our sensations
(UGG, p. 304). The essential role which the senses play in the
discernment of beauty is both recognized and encouraged. For

König, all rules or principles of art are based in the agreement between the qualities of the object and their effect which is based in our experience of them. Beauty, then, is not simply in the eye of the beholder, but also resides in the object itself. Object and subject must be in perfect agreement if perfection is actually present and the creation of this agreement determines true art.

Drawing upon Rollin's De la maniere d'enseigner et d'étudier les belles lettres of 1726, König concludes his essay by praising the merits of "eine ausbündige und zarte Empfindung" which is sensitively aware of the true beauty of Nature. This "glückliche Fähigkeit" unites both the impressions received through sensation and the judgment of the understanding, remaining "sparsam und vorsichtig mitten im Uberfluss (UGG, p. 319)! Error in aesthetic judgment is attributable to a deficiency in this refined sensation and is perceived as the cause of all corruptible writing, wherein "der Witz von der Urtheilungs-Krafft entblöst ist, und sich durch den Schein des Schönen betrügen läst" (Quintilian) (UGG, p. 320).

It is König's deepest conviction that by uniting sensation with the understanding a new and more objective standard of Taste can be achieved whereby "die unveränderlichen Regeln des schönen und des wahren" (UGG, p. 321) can be comprehended and applied to the judgment of genuine works of art. The true literary critic will express his aesthetic judgment with proofs and examples from ancient and modern, foreign and domestic poets and orators alike (UGG, p. 322). The final result of

König's discussion of good Taste thus results in the call for a sounder methodology in the evaluation of works of art.

What, then, was König's stance on the issue of good Taste? In König's investigation, "Verstand" and "Erfahrung", "Empfindung" and "Begriff", objective and subjective Taste are synthesized to create impeccable Taste. In so doing, König draws directly upon the rhetorical tradition. As he notes, both Quintilian and Cicero, in order to better express the nature of good Taste, spoke of a combination of ratio and voluntas, of reason and emotion (UGG, p. 292). Nature and art must then be united in order to gain the ideal of perfect Taste (UGG, p. 270). In this way, relativism was transcended and aesthetic judgment gained objectivity.

III. Gottsched's Analysis of Good Taste

The third chapter of the Versuch einer Critischen Dichtkunst is entitled, "Vom guten Geschmack eines Poeten". Gottsched opens this chapter by stating that his task will be to explain, in his own way, the general rule that a poet must have good Taste (VCD, I 99). In noting the prevalence of the question of what constitutes good Taste in the early Eighteenth Century, Gottsched leaves the discussion of the origin of its contemporary understanding to others, most notably to König and Bodmer.

> Das haben schon andre vor mir gethan,
> deren Schrifften ich mit Vergnügen und
> Vortheil gelesen habe (:darunter ich
> denn des Hrn. Geh. Secr. Königs und
> Hrn. Bodmers aus Zürich dahin gehörige

Sachen, nahmhafft machen und loben muss)
(VCD, p. 99).

Curiously enough, that which we have included in parentheses
was then deleted in later editions of the Critische Dichtkunst[17]. This method of criticism by means of deletions and
additions occurs a number of times throughout later editions of
Gottsched's critical poetics and is particularly striking whenever Gottsched discusses good Taste and beauty.

Like Bodmer (VEK, p. 17), Gottsched uses the term, "der
metaphorische Geschmack" (VCD, p. 101), an expression which
reveals the recent application of the term to aesthetic judgment. Like König (UGG, pp. 300, 316), Gottsched takes issue
with the favorite saying of the day: "Vom Geschmacke müsse
man nicht viel zancken" (VCD, p. 101).

The thrust of Gottsched's consideration of Taste and
beauty is to establish, in opposition to any relativistic
interpretation, an objective standard. And he attempts to do
so by way of logical deduction.

Gottsched points out that people who judge according to
"dem blossen Geschmack" often contradict each other, and
insists that, since both judgments cannot possibly be true,
"dasjenige Urtheil dem andern vorzuziehen sey, so mit den
Regeln der Baukunst und dem Ausspruche eines Meisters in dieser
Wissenschaft, einstimmig ist" (VCD, p. 103). Adherence to
the rules of art, then, becomes the basic criterion in the
judgment of a work of art. And since Gottsched insists that

these rules are not the invention of man, but are grounded "in
der unveränderlichen Natur der Dinge selbst", i.e. in order and
in harmony, rules of art are therefore objective and indisput-
able (VCD, p. 103). The principles which underly art are the
result of "langwierige Erfahrung" and "vieles Nachsinnen" and
are hardly arbitrary, even when at times "jemand nach seinem
Geschmacke, demjenigen Wercke den Vorzug zugestünde, welches
dawieder mehr oder weniger verstossen hätte" (VCD, p. 104).
Although König does not admit that the specialist is the final
judge in questions of Taste, he nevertheless agrees that judgment according to the rules and principles of art renders
objectivity to aesthetic judgment.

> Alle Kunst-Regeln, die man einmahl für
> gültig angenommen, sind nicht schlechter-
> dings aus dem Gehirn ersonnen, sondern
> aus der Eigenschafft der Dinge und ihrer
> Würckungen hergeholet, von uns der Natur
> selbst abgelernet, aus der Erfahrung
> bemerckt, mit Vernunfft untersucht, und
> durch den allgemeinen Beyfall der Kenner,
> bestätiget worden (UGG, pp. 307-308).

Gottsched agrees with König that the immediate judgment
of the sensual qualities of an object is made by "die innerliche Empfindung...die [and Gottsched is not certain here]
entweder wirklich ausser uns verhanden ist, oder von unsrer
eignen Phantasie hervorgebracht worden" (VCD, p. 104). But
Gottsched is quick to turn to the understanding. In order to
assure that our aesthetic judgments are indeed good, some
critical detachment is necessary. This is the proper function
of the understanding. An example of this process would be that

of a painter who first creates an image of an object in his mind through his senses and who then judges the beauty of the image with the aid of the understanding.

Gottsched demands that whoever possesses good Taste must judge correctly "von der klar empfundenen Schönheit eines Dinges" (VCD, p. 105). He then reiterates his claim that the true "Probierstein" for this is to be found "in den Regeln der Vollkommenheit" which are obvious in the works of art themselves and in the judgment of specialists. Good Taste, then, is that which conforms to the rules of art, "die von der Vernunft in einer Art von Sachen allbereit festgesetzet worden" (VCD, p. 105). In the realm of poetry, good Taste is defined as:

> ...eine Geschicklichkeit von der Schönheit
> eines Gedichtes, Gedanckens oder Ausdruckes
> recht zu urtheilen, die man gröstentheils
> nur klar empfunden, und nach den Regeln
> selbst nicht geprüfet hat (VCD, p. 105).
> [emphasis mine]

Sound aesthetic judgment, through the uniting of sensation and understanding, will be able to render judgments of beauty which have the same validity as rules of art.

A frequent question of the day was whether Taste was something in-born or acquired through learning. According to Gottsched, we bring only "die blosse Fähigkeit" of Taste into the world (VCD, p. 105). Each of us, then, possesses the capacity to judge the beauty of sensual things. Taste "ist also dem Menschen so was natürliches als seine übrige Gemüths-

Kräffte" (VCD, p. 106). But since it is unrefined in its
natural state, it must be "erweckt, angeführt, von Fehlern
gesäubert, und auf dem guten Wege so lange erhalten werden,
bis sie ihres Thuns gewiss wird" (VCD, p. 106).

The reason for the divergence of opinion in matters of
Taste is because of education. Convinced, as Aristotle was,
that children simply imitate the habits and mannerisms of
their parents and teachers, Gottsched, quite pompously we
might add, insists that our judgments of Taste simply reflect
the prevalent attitudes of our social class. And since the
majority of people are underprivileged and have simply not had
a proper education, this is "die erste Quelle des übeln
Geschmackes, der in den meisten Ländern noch so allgemein ist"
(VCD, p. 107). Gottsched's elitism on the subject goes without
saying.

How then can good Taste be advanced? "Nichts anders als
der Gebrauch der gesunden Vernunft" (VCD, p. 107).

> Man halte nichts vor schön oder hesslich,
> weil man es so nennen gehöret, oder weil
> die Leute die man kennet, es davor halten;
> sondern man untersuche es an und vor sich,
> ob es so sey. Man muss seine eigne fünf
> Sinne zu Rathe ziehen:... (VCD, p. 107).

And this critical detachment, in Gottsched's estimation, is
what made the Greeks so great. "Alles philosophirte daselbst:
alles urtheilte frey, und folgte seinem eigenen Kopfe" (VCD,
p. 107). Through observation it was discovered that order and
harmony brought forth perfection and that where obscurity and
confusion reigned there was dissatisfaction and abuse (VCD,

p. 108). The "Tiefsinnigen" among the Greeks were then able to ascertain what rules or principles were in operation when perfection was present.

> Also hat man zu aller Zeit gesehen, dass
> die Regeln der Griechen, in allen freyen
> Künsten, die beste Anleitung zum guten
> Geschmacke gewesen sind (VCD, p. 108).

In order to avoid confusion, it is necessary to understand that the Greeks for Gottsched serve only as initiators ("Anleiter") in the cultivation of Taste, and that it is the exercise of Reason which accounts for their success. Gottsched's hope is that the German people emulate the Greeks in this respect and thereby gain an equivalent depth of understanding in aesthetic concerns. What Germany was so desperately lacking at this time, however, was a vibrant national literature which was vital to the cultivation and refinement of Taste. For good literature, as the work of Opitz is said to demonstrate (VCD, p. 109), will encourage good Taste. But since Germany had a long way to go in this respect, Gottsched could do no other than recommend the reading of the great masters of European literature. What work, then, should a young man read for the development of good Taste?

> Terentz, Vergil, Horatz, von den Lateinern;
> Petrarcha und Tasso von Italienern; Malherbe,
> Boileau, Corneille, Racine, Molière und
> Voltaire von Franzosen; Heins und Cats von
> Holländern; Opitz, Dach, Flemming, Tscherning,
> beyde Gryphier, Amthor, Canitz und Günther von
> unsern Landesleuten: (VCD, p. 109).

Instruction into the true merits and shortcomings of these prestigious writers was seen as an important step in the cultivation of good Taste in Germany.

Near the end of his chapter on Taste, Gottsched shifts his attention from the perception to the very nature of beauty. And he begins this section by addressing himself to the question of whether or not a writer should poeticize in accordance with the general Taste of his time and place. Why, for instance, should we read the Greeks and not encourage that which pleases us in the here and now?

Gottsched's answer is based on the assumption that since natural objects are beautiful works of art the artist should imitate and emulate their beauty. Correspondence with beautiful Nature is "die Quelle aller Schönheit".

> Die Schönheit eines künstlichen Werckes
> beruht nicht auf einem leeren Dünckel;
> sondern hat ihren festen und nothwendigen
> Grund in der Natur der Dinge. Gott hat
> alles nach Zahl, Maass und Gewicht
> geschaffen. Die natürlichen Dinge sind
> (an sich selber) schön; und wenn also
> die Kunst auch was schönes hervor bringen
> will, muss sie dem Muster der Natur
> nachahmen. Das genaue Verhältniss, die
> Ordnung und richtige Abmessung aller Theile
> daraus ein Ding besteht, ist die Quelle
> der (aller) Schönheit. Die Nachahmung der
> (vollkommenen) Natur, kan also einem
> künstlichen Wercke die Vollkommenheit geben,
> dadurch es dem Verstande gefällig und
> angenehm wird (:und die Abweichung von
> ihrem Muster, wird allemal etwas ungestaltes
> und abgeschmacktes zuwege bringen) (VCD,
> p. 110; 4th edition, p. 132).

The addition of intensifiers (noted in parentheses) is indeed illuminating in later editions of Gottsched's work. The first addition involves the notion of an sich, that is, an a priori assumption concerning beauty which is by nature logical or rational in the strictest sense. It clearly reveals Gottsched's insistence upon an objective standard of beauty. The second intensifier makes Gottsched's pronouncements even more general and the third reveals (as later in the Handlexikon) the idea that the artist must creatively imitate beautiful Nature in all its splendor. The last addition to his statement stands as a warning to all those who would mock the idea that nature itself, perfect and whole, must be the model for the creative production of poetic works of art.

In the Weltweisheit of 1733, beauty is said to embrace both order and perfection. That beauty embraces order follows from the premise: "Ein jedes Ding hat Ordnung, und folglich Wahrheit in sich" (EGW, P. 262, p. 221). The close proximity of beauty to truth is already implied. That beauty embraces perfection is clearly stated.

> Die Vollkommenheit ist also die Uebereinstimmung
> des Mannichfaltigen...Wenn eine solche Vollkommenheit
> in die Sinne fällt, und, ohne deutlich eingesehen
> zu werden, nur klar empfunden wird, so heisst sie
> eine Schönheit (EGW, p. 220).

By concentrating on the order and perfection of beautiful objects, Gottsched attempts to attribute to his concept of beauty and Taste the certainty and objectivity of the mathematical sciences (VCD, p. 111). In the final analysis, the Taste of experts takes precedence over the Taste of a nation:

> Nicht der Beyfall macht eine Sache schön;
> sondern die Schönheit erwirbt sich bey
> Verständigen den Beyfall (VCD, p. 111).

The suggestion of Bodmer and later Breitinger that the artist
should follow the Taste of his time and place is simply not
accepted by Gottsched.

> Wenn man die Reste von ihren [the Greeks]
> Meisterstücken dargegen hält, wird man
> gewiss finden, dass sie eine Schönheit
> an sich haben, die der Vernunft nothwendig
> gefallen muss, (wenn sie nur nicht in
> Vorurtheilen ersoffen, und in seine eigene
> Misgeburten allbereit verliebet ist. Dieses
> thun insgemein diejenigen, die ein tief-
> gewurzeltes Vorurtheil für ihre Nation,
> oder für ihre Zeiten haben, und sich
> einbilden, ein jedes Volk habe seinen
> eigenen Geschmack, und jedes Jahrhundert
> auch. Da könnte nun dasjenige hier schön
> seyn, was dort hässlich ist. Doch davon
> will ich weiter unten reden) (VCD, 4th
> edition, p. 130).

It is obvious that this addition constitutes a direct criticism
of Breitinger's remarks. To my knowledge, this constitutes
the first open debate on the question of the relativity of
beauty in Germany.

Presupposing an objective standard of beauty, Gottsched
makes a clear distinction between true ("wahre") and imagined
("eingebildete") beauty.

> Aber es giebt wahre, es giebt auch
> eingebildete Schönheiten. Diese
> erwecken freylich bey vielen eine
> Belustigung; aber nur so lange, als
> sie dieselben vor Schönheiten ansehen.
> Offtmahls lernen sie begreifen, dass
> sie sich in ihrem Urtheile betrogen;
> und alsdann erwecket ihnen dasjenige
> Verdruss, was ihnen vorher wohlgefiel.
> Von ferne sieht offt eine Person sehr
> wohl aus; wenn wir sie aber in der Nähe
> erblicken, ist sie hesslich...(VCD, p. 112).

The question of beauty, then, also involves the problem of

appearance and reality. This is quite similar to the more
problematical account of the same in <u>Die</u> <u>Discourse</u> <u>der</u> <u>Mahlern</u>,
where deceptive is differentiated from genuine beauty. An
apparent beauty, says Gottsched, is simply "ein Zusammenfluss
unzehlicher Ungereimtheiten" (<u>VCD</u>, p. 113). Since beauty can
be illusory, it follows that Taste can also be called into
question. Therefore, in Gottsched's opinion, the luxury of
knowing what constitutes good Taste and beautiful things is
afforded only by a select few.

> So müssen sich denn die Poeten niemahls
> nach dem Geschmacke der Welt, das ist
> des grossen Haufens, oder unverständigen
> Pöbels richten. Dieser vielköpfigte
> Götze urtheilet offt sehr verkehrt von
> Dingen (<u>VCD</u>, p. 113).

Genuine artists, then, have the function of discerning and
disseminating beauty through their work in accordance with
their own good Taste.

In summarizing, we must assess the merits and limitations
of Gottsched's concept of Taste. Whereas theology and ethics
were the sources of König's understanding of Taste, Gottsched's
concepts of Taste and beauty have their basis in logic. It is
by way of logical deduction that Gottsched can assume that an
objective standard of Taste exists. For an instant, Gottsched's
consideration of Taste seems to include König's synthesis of
sensation and understanding. Yet, by insisting that Reason
and ultimate adherence to the rules of art constitute the only
acceptable criteria of objective judgment, Gottsched upsets the
balance created by König and lays the greater emphasis upon the

understanding in the perception of beauty. Although he admits that beauty is essentially a "je ne sais quoi", Gottsched is not content with the fact and concentrates upon the harmony and order which are characteristic of beauty and perfection. In this way, he is the most neo-classic of the early Aufklärer.

Rather than assign good Taste to some imaginative sixth sense as the Abbé Dubos had done, König and Gottsched attribute it primarily to the working of the understanding, and thereby upgrade its objectivity. Gottsched is also in basic agreement with König's point that Taste, although a capacity common to all men, can be perfected and refined through observation, practice and instruction. This mediation between extremes is typical of all the major essays on Taste among the early Aufklärer.

Rather than attack Gottsched for his obviously elitist attitude, as the many opponents of the Gottsched Circle were fond of doing, we must question whether or not Gottsched was correct in his pronouncements. One serious question must be raised with respect to Gottsched's allegedly objective standard of Taste.

Gottsched's suggestion that the expert in matters of art must be the final judge of beauty completely overlooks the fact that such specialists themselves often disagree. So that the amount, or even the quality of education seems to have little to do with the problem of relativity of judgment. Gottsched's point, "dass man, sonderlich in sinnlichen Dingen, nach un- deutlich, oder gar dunkel erkannten Regeln, von dem, was schön oder vollkommen ist, sehr ungleich und oft auch sehr unrichtig urtheilet" (EGW, P. 258, pp. 220-221), is just as true of specialists as it is of the so-called masses. This problem is finally dealt with in the Sixth Letter of Bodmer's Neue Critische Briefe of 1749, entitled, "Von dem verschiedenen Geschmack an gleich schönen Schriften"[18], which Bodmer attributes to "die natürliche Verschiedenheit der Complexion, des Temperaments, der Sinnesart" (NCB, 6, p. 45) and the like, Gottsched, then, instead of solving the problem of relativity, has simply circumvented it.

It is now obvious that Gottsched desired an objective standard of Taste and beauty, but that he undermined his call for Reason in the discernment of beautiful objects by insisting that final judgment was determined on the basis of the authority of the expert.

IV. Breitinger's Discussion of Taste

In contrast to Gottsched, the thread of relativism which was first visible in Die Discourse der Mahlern is again obvious in Breitinger's critical poetics of 1740.

> Was nun insbesondere die nach Zeit und Ort
> so verschiedenen Gewohnheiten, Sitten,
> Gebräuche, und Meinungen ganzer Völcker
> anbelanget, so muss man freylich gestehen,
> dass das poetische Schöne in dieser Absicht
> am wenigsten an eine besondere Zeit oder
> Ort kan gebunden und festgestellet werden,
> alldieweil diese Sachen durch ihre stete
> Veränderung den Begriff von dem Schönen,
> und den Preiss des verwundersamen Neuen
> in diesem Stücke zugleich mitverändern.
> Was zu einer Zeit vor schön, anständig
> und verwundersam gehalten worden, das kan

> bey geänderten Sitten in Vergleichung
> mit neuen Begriffen von dem Schönen einen
> einen gantz widrigen Eindruck machen
> (CD, I, 126).

Poetic beauty, for Breitinger, as for Addison, Muratori, Dubos and Baumgarten, varies not only from culture to culture, but throughout time. It is therefore incumbent upon the artist to work within his own time and in his own place in accordance with the prevalent notions of Taste. His art must be an expression, then, of the aesthetic values of his own country. Indeed, this thought foreshadows the historical relativism of Sturm und Drang, which we find elaborated in Herder's Auch eine Philosophie der Geschichte zur Bildung der Menschheit (1774):

> Jede Nation hat ihren Mittelpunkt der
> Glückseligkeit in sich, wie jede
> Kugel ihren Schwerpunkt[19].

In direct opposition to Gottsched, Breitinger, in the 12th Chapter of his work, entitled, "Von der Wahl der Umstände und ihrer Verbindung", denies that Taste can be learned through the study of the rules of art.

> Darum ist es auch unmöglich, dass der gute
> Geschmack durch Regeln, die ein vollständiges
> Systema der Kunst ausmachen, gelehret und
> vorgetragen werde, weil seine Urtheile sich
> auf besondere Stellen beziehen, die nach
> ihren besondern Absichten, und nach der
> Beschaffenheit besonderer Dinge beurtheilet
> werden müssen (CD, p. 430).

Taste seems to be more of an intuitive or instinctual capacity. For it is here defined as:

> ...eine Kraft des Verstandes...welche uns
> einestheils in der Wahl besonderer Dinge
> und Umstände also leitet, dass wir alles

> dasjenige vermeiden und auslassen, was der
> vorgenommenen Materie und unsren besondern
> Absichten nachtheilig und widrig seyn mögte,
> hingegen alles aufsuchen und zusammentragen,
> was dieselben nur einigermassen befödern kan;
> eine Kraft, die uns anderntheils auch in der
> Verbindung der ausgelesenen Dinge und Umstände
> statt eines Compasses dienet, vermittelst
> dessen wir denen zwo Klippen, dem Gemeinen
> und dem Unglaublichen, zwischen denen das
> poetische Schöne lieget, und an welche es
> ziemlich nahe gräntzet, glücklich entgehen
> können. (CD, pp. 430-431).

"Dieses wehlende Urtheil", then, is the principle agent in the artistic assimilation of "das Wahrscheinliche" and "das Wunderbare" in works of art (CD, p. 431). Although a power of the understanding, Taste is far more intuitive than rational for Breitinger.

Like in Die Discourse der Mahlern, Breitinger concedes that the presence of the distasteful or ugly in a work of art can excite a pleasurable sensation within the beholder. This thought is recorded in the fourth chapter of Aristotle's Poetics, and Breitinger does not fail to quote the relevant passage from Aristotle in his chapter, "Von der Nachahmung der Natur".

> 'Etliche Urbilder...als abscheuliche Thiere,
> Todte; oder Sterbende, die wir in der Natur
> nicht anschauen dörften, oder die wir nicht
> ohne Widerwillen oder mit Schrecken anschauen
> würden, sehen wir mit Ergetzen im Gemählde,
> und je geschickter sie nachgeahmet sind, je
> mit grösserm Ergetzen betrachten wir sie (CD, p. 69).

Breitinger then comments:

> Also werden uns die strengen Leidenschaften
> des Schreckens und des Mitleidens erträglich,
> ja angenehm, wenn sie durch eine geschickte
> Nachahmung in unsrer Brust hervorgebracht
> werden (CD, p. 69).

So the presence of the distasteful is afforded a place within
the aesthetic theory of the early German Aufklärung, primarily
because of the persuasiveness of the argument that the essence
of art consists in the imitation of nature. Since art is not
nature, the ugly can even stimulate a pleasurable response in
the beholder of a work of art. On the question of art and
nature, then, neither Bodmer, nor Breitinger fail to separate
the two. This allowance for the distasteful in art precedes
the same admission by Johann Elias Schlegel in 1745: "man kann
sie nicht hinweglassen, ohne den Menschen die lebhaftesten
Vorstellungen zu rauben"[20].

In summary, although Breitinger defines Taste as a power
of understanding, it is essentially an intuitive feeling for the
proper relations between things. Poetic beauty, although relative with respect to culture and time, gains a certain objectivity when Breitinger, in agreement with Dacier, maintains that
the artist should work in accordance with the Taste of his time
and place. The following "gute Ammerskung" is from Dacier:

> 'Virgil...hat nicht alle Sachen vor brauchbar
> gehalten, die Homerus gebraucht hat, denn
> etwas, das in dem Weltalter des griechischen
> Poeten verwundersam war, hätte zu Augusts Zeit
> übel mögen aufgenommen werden, darum muss ein
> Poet seine Erdichtungen nach der Gemüths-Art,
> dem Naturell, den Gewohnheiten und Sitten
> seiner Zeit und seines Landes einrichten'
> (CD, pp. 126-127).

This is one of the three points of disagreement between
Breitinger and Gottsched on the question of Taste and beauty.

Breitinger further disagrees with Gottsched on the function

of the rules of art. For Breitinger, Taste cannot be acquired
with the aid of rules of art, a thought which is most consistent
with his definition of Taste as intuition.

The final and most important point at which Breitinger and
Gottsched part company is the question of the portrayal of
distasteful occurrences within the work of art itself. For
Gottsched, the artist must creatively imitate "die schöne
Natur" in all its splendid perfection. For Breitinger, as for
Bodmer (DM), pleasure plays a more essential role in the appreciation of art and can be derived from any successful imitation,
no matter what the object of that imitation may be. It therefore follows that the incorporation of the distasteful into the
aesthetic experience must be allowed.

The essential difference between Gottsched and Bodmer and
Breitinger on the question of beauty, then, lies in whether the
beauty of a work of art is to be found in the aesthetic quality
of the natural object itself (Gottsched), or in the artistic
imitation (Bodmer/Breitinger). Since there is no bridging this
gap, Gottsched and Bodmer and Breitinger were not able to agree
on the nature of a beautiful work of art.

V.   Bodmer and the Critische Briefe

Inspired by Addison's account of the "Great" in the
Spectator and his own concept of "das Wunderbare" in his defense of Milton, Bodmer, in the Third Critical Letter of the
Critische Briefe of 1746, offers the first comprehensive account
of the sublime in Germany.[21]

The true significance of the sublime experience lies in its transcendence both of the distasteful and evil and of the feeling of human limitation. For in the portrayal of the sublime, the creator, as well as the beholder, loses all sense of the "I" and feels the pulsating and overwhelming presence of reality in its totality. In experiencing the sublime, one encompasses all times and all ages within the here and now. To experience sublimity, then, is to sense the underlying reality of all things in the present moment, which, by virtue of the fact that sublimity includes and yet transcends the experience of the immediate world, also involves the transcendence of the seemingly finite nature of things and the limitations of the world of experience.

In the Third Critical Letter, Bodmer clearly states that "die Verwunderung" is the true "Frucht des Erhabenen" (CB, p. 95). He is quick to point out, however, that this awe or amazement is not "die Verwunderung der Menge, welche alles bewundert, grosses oder kleines, was ihr die Augen füllt, oder was ihr seltsam und neu vorkommt" (CB, p. 95). This "gemeine Verwunderung hat die Unwissenheit zur Mutter" (CB, p. 95). What Bodmer is referring to is "eine ganz andere Verwunderung, aus welcher die grösten Geister die mit dem erlauchtesten Verstande begabet sind, sich eine Ehre machen" (CB, p. 96). Much in the manner of Gottsched, Bodmer is quick to dismiss the ignorance of the "masses" on this question.

> Die Verwunderung des Pöbels ist nur ein
> dummes Angaffen, ein blindes Ueberraschen,

ohne Nachdenken und Tiefsinnigkeit
(CB, p. 96)[22].

Truly "grosse Geister" (enlightened individuals), however, are awe-struck only by the perception of the miraculous workings of nature behind or within the world of appearances. Such astonishment is awakened only "mit einem tiefen Nachsinnen" (CB, p. 96). It is therefore rational.

> Ihre Verwunderung ist demnach vernünftig,
> indem sie eben aus der Betrachtung der
> Dinge und ihrer Zusammenfügung entsteht
> (CB, p. 96).

But this state of awe can be experienced only very rarely, "weil sie [enlightened individuals] sich weder durch den Schein der Dinge, noch durch Wahn betrügen lassen, wie der Pöbel, sondern gewohnt sind, bis auf den Grund der Sachen durchzudringen; so dass sie den wahren Werth derselben kennen" (CB, p. 96).

How, then, does the sublime manifest itself? The sublime is that--

> ...welches einen hohen und sonderbaren Grad
> der Verwunderung verursacht, wie diejenige ist,
> welche die Seele mit einem feyerlichen Vergnügen
> erfüllt, wenn sie das Grosse und Ungemeine
> betrachtet, dieses liege nun in den Werken der
> Natur, als in unbegränzten Aussichten, stürmischen
> Seen, erstaunlichen Bergen, oder in wunderbaren
> Handlungen der Menschen, als in heftigen und
> begeisterten Gemüthsbewegungen, hohen Proben der
> Grossmuth und Dapferkeit, oder in Gesinnungen,
> welche sich über die gewöhnliche Beschaffenheit
> des menschlichen Gemüthes erheben (CB, pp. 94-95).

This explanation of the sublime is remarkably similar to Addison's statement on the "Great" in the 412th Number of The Spectator for June 23, 1712. Addison:

> By Greatness, I do not only mean the Bulk of
> any single Object, but the Largeness of a

> whole View, considered as one entire Piece.
> Such are the Prospects of an open Champian
> Country, a vast uncultivated Desart, of huge
> Heaps of Mountains, high Rocks and Precipices,
> or a wide Expanse of Waters, where we are not
> struck with the Novelty or Beauty of the Sight,
> but with that rude kind of Magnificence which
> appears in many of these stupendous Works of
> Nature (<u>Spectator</u>, p. 66).

"Greatness", for Addison, is particularly fascinating, for

> ...our Imagination loves to be filled with
> an Object, or to grasp at any thing that is
> too big for its Capacity. We are flung into
> a pleasing Astonishment at such unbounded
> Views, and feel a delightful Stilness and
> Amazement in the Soul at the Apprehension of
> them (<u>Spectator</u>, p. 66).

For Addison, the "Great" is pleasing primarily because it

awakens a sense of freedom from restraint within us:

> ...a spacious Horizon is an Image of Liberty,
> where the Eye has Room to range abroad, to
> expatiate at large on the Immensity of its
> Views, and to lose it self amidst the Variety
> of Objects that offer themselves to its
> Observation (<u>Spectator</u>, p. 66).

The incorporation of the sublime into the work of art,

then, gives rise to "heftige und begeisterte Gemüthsbewegungen"

which enable the beholder to transcend "die gewöhnliche

Beschaffenheit des menschlichen Gemüthes". It is this feeling

of <u>freedom</u> <u>from</u> <u>restraint</u> which grants to man an awareness of

the dynamics and power of Nature and a feeling of momentary

transcendence of his world and of his own finitude. The

accomplishment of this end characterizes the genuine work of art.

Of special importance to Bodmer's theory are the great

personages of history.

> Aber unter der grossen Anzahl der Menschen
> kan man wider von Zeit zu Zeit etliche wenige

> wahrnehmen, welche sich durch ihre Denkungsart,
> durch ihre Lebensregeln, durch ihre Thaten,
> von der Menge sondern, welche·die Gebraüche,
> und die gemeine Regeln verlassen dieselben
> grossmüthig bestreiten und ihren eigenen Trieben
> folgen dürfen. Diese Menschen werden denn
> wunderbar und erstaunlich; sie verfallen auf die
> Tugend oder das Laster; ihr grosses Gemüthe
> zeige sich durch Würkungen, Thaten, oder
> durch Worte. Es scheint, dass sie die
> menschliche Natur übersteigen, und man
> wundert sich, wie es seyn könne, dass
> Menschen sich zu so hohen Entschlüssen
> und Thaten, die so übermenschlich oder
> unmenschlich scheinen, erheben können
> (CB, pp. 99-100).

Now Bodmer's statement here bears only a remote resemblance to
Hegel's philosophy of history. Although Bodmer is obviously
referring to those "weltgeschichtliche Individuen", such as
Julius Caeser, who operate in accordance to their own drives
and ambitions irrespective of the forces against them, his
purpose here is not to illustrate the workings of any type of
Weltgeist which, with the unfolding of history, gains ever
greater awareness of itself as free. But rather, Bodmer is
developing a theory of the sublime and of a sublime style for
inclusion into literary works of art, most specifically into
that of drama.

The power of the sublime is so great for Bodmer that its
effects can be felt even outside the works of nature and art
and quite apart from art's utility as an instructive and de-
lightful medium of expression.

> Wenn wir die Augen weiter in die Welt herum
> gehen lassen, so werden wir neben diesen
> Werken der Natur und der Kunst gewisse grosse
> Würkungen wahrnehmen, deren Zweck nicht ist
> zu unterrichten oder zu ergetzen, sondern

> lediglich den Menschen in Bestürzung, in
> Schrecken, in Mitleiden zu setzen. Die einen
> haben Gott zum Urheber, andere den Menschen
> und noch andere die übrigen freyen Wesen
> (CB, p. 98).

Here, then, lie the seeds for a theory of the sublime as found,

for example, in Schiller's dramatic theory. Schiller's defini-

tion of the sublime in his essay, "Vom Erhabenen" (1793) is

essentially the same as that of Bodmer:

> Erhaben nennen wir ein Objekt, bei dessen
> Vorstellung unsre sinnliche Natur ihre
> Schranken, unsre vernünftige Natur aber
> ihre Überlegenheit, ihre Freiheit von
> Schranken fühlt...[23]

The proper function of art, then, is no longer only that of

instruction or the arousal of pleasure, but also the moving of

the beholder with the overpowering sublimity of Nature. This is

the decisive point at which poetic enthusiasm, creative imagina-

tion and the experience of the sublime combine to render the

most powerful Wirkungsästhetik before Lessing and the Sturm

und Drang writers. Art is now perceived as an autonomous realm

of experience, subject only to its own laws.

What, then, is the special province of the sublime?

> Wir sehen also deutlich genug, was das für
> Sachen seyn, welche mit Recht erhaben genannt
> werden; es sind nämlich die grossen Würkungen
> und Thaten der freyen Wesen, denen der
> Charakter eines grossen Gemüthes eingepräget
> ist, welche die menschlichen Kräfte zu
> übersteigen scheinen, und vermögend sind, in
> Erstaunen, in tiefes Nachsinnen, in Furcht
> und Schrecken zu setzen, und das Mitleiden
> auf einem hohen Grade rege zu machen (CB, p. 101).

Drawing both upon the rhetorical tradition and upon the

aesthetics of Dubos with their emphasis upon the moving of the

beholder, Bodmer could develop a theory of literature which
was centered upon the arousal of fear, pity and empathy some
ten years prior to either Mendelssohn or Lessing. The insistence,
then, by many critics that the merits of sentiment were not fully
realized until around 1755 in Germany is to overlook the obvious
importance of human emotion among the early Aufklärer.

With the aid of Longinus's On the Sublime, which appeared
again in the eighteenth century, "Bodmer-Longinus", as Heinrich
Füssli was to name him[24], developed a theory of an "erhabene
Schreibart" which was to have a profound effect on the later
eighteenth century in Germany. It is this sublime style which
now enhances the work of the artist and enables him to stir the
emotions of the beholder as never before.

> In diesem Falle werden seine erhabene
> Beschreibungen allemal das Gemüthe der
> Leser mit starken Gedanken und grossen
> Bewegungen anfüllen, Entzückung, Schrecken,
> Mitleiden, Hochachtung, Abscheu, werden
> beständig damit verknüpfet seyn. Und diese
> Regungen sind eben die Kennzeichen der
> erhabenen Schreibart; wenn sie dieselben
> erreget, so thue man ohne Furcht den
> Ausspruch, dass sie erhaben sey; ist dieses
> nicht, so kan man versichert seyn, dass
> nur der Schein des Erhabenen vorhanden ist
> (CB, pp. 101-102).

Upon concluding his Third Critical Letter, Bodmer offers a
miniature aesthetic system, or structure, which I have cate-
gorized as follows:

FACULTIES	PSYCHO-AESTHETIC QUALITIES	AIMS
Herz	das Erhabene - das Grosse - eine hohe Natur	Bewunderung
Witz	das Scharfsinnige - das Schöne - einen schönen Geist	Ergötzen
Verstand	das Tiefsinnige - das Wahre - ein gesundes Urtheil	Überzeugung

The art of combining these three faculties, then, characterizes the genuine artist, whereas the literary critic appraises a work of art on the basis of all aesthetic qualities combined. In establishing these criteria, a greater objectivity could be arrived at in the discernment of good Taste and beauty within literature. Works of art were no longer to be assessed in light of their conformity with accepted rules, but rather on the basis of their aesthetic quality and effect.

Let us summarize our findings:

For Leibniz, all aesthetic knowledge belongs to the second of four grades of knowledge[25]. Our perception of beauty, then, is a form of clear ("klar") but confused ("verworren") knowledge in which natural phenomena, such as colors, are clearly perceived but nonetheless remain intellectually indistinct. In Leibniz's estimation, Taste, as distinguished from understanding, is a "je ne sais quoi", which, although immediately recognizable, escapes adequate definition.

Insofar as all of the early Aufklärer recognized the ultimate elusiveness of Taste, they were in essential agreement with Shaftesbury (1671-1713) and Hutcheson (1694-1746), who perceived of Taste as an indeterminable sense independent of Reason[26]. Yet, the German critics of the early eighteenth century were not content in leaving this fundamentally instinctual sense for beauty on the level of sensation. As we have seen, they endeavored to afford Taste some degree of objectivity, either by basing that feeling on the general consensus of an entire nation, or by appealing to the understanding and tradition. Where Bodmer and Breitinger agreed with Dacier that the work of art should reflect the general Taste of a nation's people, König and Gottsched attempted to ground Taste on the dictates of the understanding and the rules of art. Taste, then, may begin as an "I know not what", but, in the final analysis, it was required to prove its feeling for the beautiful by way of rational demonstration. The net result of this need for certainty is that feeling must make an account of itself before the tribunal of understanding--a thought which is diametrically opposed to that of David Hume (1711-1776)[27]. In this way, the writer, in adhering to the demands of good Taste, was able to transcend relativism and attain a greater degree of objectivity.

Since it is easier to feel than to critically assess the beauty of an object (König), time was required for a more objective evaluation of the merits of a work of art. Our first assessment of a beautiful object, then, is purely physiological, whereas the later judgment is the more consciously developed. As R. Saisselin informs us, this was also

Batteux's position: "Le Goût doit être un sentiment qui nous avertit si la belle Nature est bien ou mal imitée"[28].

Now since this was the understanding of the early German Aufklärer already in the 1720's and 1730's, the theory of imitation found in the Abbé Batteux's Les Beaux-Arts réduits à un même principe of 1746, which was translated in part by Gottsched in 1754[29] and in full by Johann Adolf Schlegel in 1759[30], cannot be assumed to be yet another borrowing from foreign sources, but rather the confirmation of what the Germans had already intuited and expressed concerning the need for an objective standard of Taste. Furthermore, it was not until 1756 that Edmund Burke (1729?-1797) lended greater objectivity to Taste by affirming the essential role of understanding and the rules of art in his A Philosophical Enquiry Into the Origin of our Ideas of the Sublime and the Beautiful. As is now obvious, the Germans had expressed this need some thirty years prior to Burke's essay. This search for kinship and confirmation was typical of everything the Germans did in the area of poetics and aesthetics. It is a position which has been too long overlooked and mistakenly interpreted as a lack of originality on the part of the German Aufklärer.

Although the early Aufklärer, like the French and the English, endeavored to cultivate good Taste in their own country, they were unable to agree on important questions. Where does beauty reside, for instance? In the natural object, as Gottsched and Baumgarten assumed? Or does beauty lie in the artistic imitation, like Bodmer and Breitinger insisted. And

how great a role should the understanding or authority play
in the final determination of the correctness of aesthetic
judgment? All this is made even more problematical when one
considers the great differences of opinion among the early
enlightened critics concerning the Taste of their own works.
Immanuel Pyra's Erweis, dass die Gottschedianische Sekte den
Geschmack verderbe (1743-1744)[31] and Georg Friedrich Meier's
Beurtheilung der Gottschedischen Dichtkunst (1747)[32] are
living examples of these differences. For both of these
writers, Gottsched's Critische Dichtkunst was, in effect
an even greater ill than the poetry of the Second Silesian
School, as, for instance, Meier suggests:

> Da ich nun die Gottschedische Dichtkunst für
> ein Buch halte, welches voller Mängel und
> Fehler ist, so halte ich dieselbe für ein
> Buch, welches den Geschmack der Deutschen
> in der Dichtkunst verdirbt (BGD, p. 4).

The question of the cultivation of Taste, was, therefore,
a heated and much discussed topic in Germany. And the reason
for this difference of opinion was no doubt attributable to the
fact that, in the final analysis, Taste is simply not veri-
fiable. What is significant, however, is that the question of
what constituted good Taste provided a lively forum for wide-
spread debate. Art in Germany was coming into its own.

Although beauty was seen to reveal the wholeness and well-
being of man within Nature and society, Bodmer soon came to
realize that the mere contemplation of beauty, and hence of
order, proportion and form, was actually ruinous for the arousal
of strong emotions. Bodmer, then, was the one, who, for the

first time in the history of German thought, clearly distinguished between beauty and pleasure--a thought which is precursory to Mendelssohn's and Kant's formulations concerning
the disinterestedness which accompanies the contemplation of
beauty, a passivity which pietistic and aesthetic contemplation have in common[33]. For this very reason, the year 1746
is decisive for the history of German aesthetics. For it now
became clear that, if literature was to achieve its end by
moving and edifying the beholder, then something far more
overpowering and awesome than imitations of beautiful nature
was needed to stir our emotions. The artistic re-creation of
the sublime thus became the true source of genuine works of art.

In developing his theory of the sublime, Bodmer found the
key to a truly effective art. The very sense of liberation and
freedom from restraint, which the human spirit seemed to cry out
for in an absolutistic age, became the great moment in literary
expression. By 1746, then, German poetics and aesthetics
underwent a decisive turn from the rules of Aristotle and Horace
to a freer and more captivating style based on enthusiasm and
the dynamic thought of Longinus. Aesthetic experience and
aesthetic judgment thus began to lose their original orientation
toward rules and became expressions of good Taste.

CONCLUSION

POETICS AND AESTHETICS OF THE EARLY AUFKLÄRER.

THE WRITER AS AN ARTIST

> Das Wahre des Verstandes gehöret
> für die Weltweisheit, hingegen
> eignet der Poet sich das Wahre
> der Einbildungskraft zu (Johann
> Jacob Breitinger).

The golden mean in the creation of literary works of art, as reflected in the major writings on poetics and aesthetics at the time of the early German Aufklärung, is one of balance between probable representation and creative freedom in the imitation of nature, poetic furor and controlled expression in the workings of the creative imagination, and sensation and understanding in the exercise of good Taste.[1] Literary excellence was thus seen to be the result of the harmonious cooperation of the creative faculties of the artist.

If there is one principle of art which best characterizes the poetic theory and practice of the day, then it must certainly be that of the imitation of nature. From this one principle all of the various rules of art and of aesthetic judgment proceeded. But what was meant by the dictum, 'imitate nature'? How was nature to be imitated? And what end does the imitation of nature serve?

These and similar questions have baffled most critics of

this period. The resultant frustration over the apparent
irresolvability of such questions has led to much misunderstanding. Representative of the attitude of many critics is
that of Franz Servaes. For Servaes (1887), the actual content of the principle of imitation is "ein wesentlich nega-
tiver": "Was in der Natur kein Vorbild hat, ist von der
Dichtung ausgeschlossen!"[2] Now such a narrow perspective,
which, we may add, was totally foreign to the minds of these
enlightened critics, cannot possibly account for the fact that
the formulation of the rule itself is sufficiently vague to allow
for all creative freedom short of improbability.

For Gottsched, the imitation of beautiful nature, which
presupposes a certain distance from reality per se, consists
in the creative poetisation of truth, "das Schöne" and "das
Wahre" being coequal. In Breitinger's understanding, the
literary artist must re-create nature in accordance with its
possible manifestations. And in the work of Johann Elias
Schlegel, there is a shift from the imitation of the pheno-
menal world alone to the projection of the world of noumena.
So that with the insight that the literary artist must no
longer be content to simply imitate the original ("Urbild")
in nature, but endeavor to bring his art into ever greater
agreement with the idea ("Begriff"/"Vorbild") which the beholder possesses of the natural object, there is a notable
development toward the subjectivization and psychological
individualization of nature on the part of the Stürmer und

Dränger.

We have seen that the imitation of nature for the early Aufklärer does not involve any sort of photographic reproduction of existent reality. The desired outcome is "poetic" realism, not naturalism S. Bing (1934) was the first to capture the essence of what these early 18th Century critics were saying: "Nachahmen", she affirms, "kann sich steigern vom Abbilden zum natürlich, naturgemäss Bilden, bis zum Erdichten"[3]. The artistic imitation of nature is a re-creative act, or, as A. Baeumler has named it, "gesetzliches Schaffen"[4].

Although Christian Wolff's definition of the Einbildungs-kraft of the artist as a solely reproductive faculty was the point of departure for the early Aufklärer, by 1740, this central creative faculty was attributed a freedom and autonomy hitherto unknown. As we have seen, this progression is most obvious in the work of Johann Bodmer. From Die Discourse der Mahlern (1721-1723) and the essay Von dem Einfluss und Gebrauche der Einbildungs-Krafft (1727) to his defense of Milton in Von dem Wunderbaren in der Poesie (1740), Bodmer gradually emancipates the creative imagination from its essentially reproductive function and assigns to it a distinctly creative role in the invention of new and possible worlds which operate in accordance with their own laws. Common to all of the early Aufklärer, however, is the thought that the imagination of the artist is allowed all freedom short of improbability.

We have found that, already in the 1720's, poetic
enthusiasm was perceived as the true stimulus behind the
"erhitzte Phantasey" of the literary artist. And Bodmer's
thought that such enthusiasm drives the poet out of his senses
is obviously tied to that of Plato's in the Ion:

> For the poet is a light and winged and holy
> thing, and there is no invention in him
> until he has been inspired and is out of
> his senses, and the mind is no longer in
> him: when he has not attained to this state,
> he is powerless and is unable to utter his
> oracles[5].

The neo-Platonic strain of thought is thus very much a part of
the poetic and aesthetic theory of the early German Aufklärung.

What, then, is the relationship between imitation and
imagination according to the early Aufklärer?

We have established that it is one of mutual cooperation[6].
Both emotional exuberance and creative imagination in the creation of lively and vibrant imagery and sensible restraint in
the maintenance of the believability, i.e. credibility of art
were required in order to produce the maximum effect of which
literature is capable. In his Critische Betrachtungen über
die Poetischen Gemählde Der Dichter (1741)[7], Bodmer's discussion
of the relationship between creative imagination and the understanding is representative of the position held by all of the
early Aufklärer. As for the Einbildungskraft:

> ...sie stellet uns nicht alleine das Würckliche
> in einem lebhaften Gemählde vor Augen, und
> macht die entferntesten Sachen gegenwärtig,
> sondern sie zieht auch mit einer mehr als
> zauberischen Kraft das, so nicht ist, aus dem

> Stande der Möglichkeit hervor, theilt ihm dem
> Scheine nach eine Würcklichkeit mit, und machet,
> dass wir diese neuen Geschöpfe gleichsam sehen,
> hören, und empfinden...(BPG, pp. 13-14).

Nonetheless, the imagination of the artist must remain within

the bounds of probability.

> Alleine, die erhitzte Phantasie, wenn sie in der
> Arbeit ihrer Schöpfung nicht durch die Weissheit
> des Verstandes geleitet wird, welcher alleine
> lehret, in was vor Mass, Zahl und Gewichte, die
> ergetzende Harmonie der Dinge bestehe, ist allzu
> geneigt über die Gräntzen des Glaubwürdigen und
> Wahrscheinlichen auszuschweifen, und sich in dem
> ungeheuren Abgrunde des Abentheurlichen zu
> verlieren, welches an das öde Reich des Unmöglichen
> gränzet, wo immerwährender Krieg und Widerspruch
> herrschet (BPG, pp. 14-15).

Perhaps the best statement on the role of Reason in the

creative process was made by Johann Andreas Cramer (1723-1788)

and Christlob Mylius in their Bemühugen zur Beförderung der

Critik und des guten Geschmacks (1743/1744)[8]:

> Ein Dichter...will die Wahrheiten mehr sinnlich
> machen, als den Verstand überzeugen: scharfe
> Erklärungen und Schlüsse sind seine Gegenstände
> nicht: er will die Einbildungskraft mit Bildern
> und Dichtungen, und den Witz mit den geistigsten
> uns sinnreichsten Einfällen unterhalten, ob die
> Wahrheit gleich überall zum Grunde lieget: Ein
> jeder erkennet daraus, dass die Einbildungskraft
> und der Witz in der Dichtkunst mehr, als die
> Kraft zu schlüssen und zu erweisen, herrsche,
> ob die Vernunft gleich dabey nicht müssig ist,
> sondern gemeldete Kräfte in Ordnung hält, dass
> sie nicht ausschweifen" (BBC, I, 34).

The beauty of a work of art is thus assured when the liveli-

ness of the imagination is coupled with the orderliness of the

understanding.

The early Aufklärer were thus united in the conviction

that the <u>creative</u> imitation of nature was essential to the advancement of a truly productive literature.

The question of good Taste was most thoroughly investigated by Johann Ulrich König. Consistent with the desire for synthesis among the early 18th Century critics in Germany, König called for a uniting of sensation and understanding in the perception of beauty. "Ein Trieb des Herzens" is united with the "Würckung des Verstandes" to create impeccable Taste. By remaining "sparsam und vorsichtig mitten im Uberfluss" (<u>UGG</u>, p. 319), good Taste gained a renewed objectivity and thus transcended the relativism of the day. Nature <u>and</u> art must then be united in the creation of genuine works of art.

Contrary to what most literary histories of Germany lead us to believe, these early enlightened critics, and artists in their own right, sharply distinguished between art and philosophy. As we have shown, both Gottsched and Breitinger insisted that the dissemination of "trockene Wahrheiten", although acceptable and necessary in philosophy, was utterly ruinous in the domain of art. Indeed, the spread of philosophy was seen as a contributing factor in the moral degeneration of man. Speaking of the tendency among Germans to revere philosophy and its "abgezogene Wahrheiten", Bodmer, in his defense of Milton (and of art <u>per se</u>), poignantly added:

> ...diese [die Philosophie] macht unsere Deutschen
> seit einiger Zeit so vernünftig und so schliessend,
> dass sie zugleich matt und tro[c]ken werden; die
> Lustbarkeiten des Verstandes haben ihr gantzes
> Gemuthe eingenommen, und diese unterdrucken die
> Lustbarkeiten der Einbildungskraft (<u>CAW</u>, p. *6).

These early Aufklärer were thus well aware that art, unlike philosophy, which was the result of rational discourse,
was essentially a manifestation of creative imagination. Poetic
truth was not rational truth: "...es kan dem Verstand etwas
falsch zu seyn düncken, das die Einbildung für wahr annimmt"
(CD, p. 138). This is why the early enlightened critics could
agree with Aristotle that a persuasive impossibility in the
realm of art was preferrable to an unpersuasive possibility
(Poetics, 1460^a).

But what, then, was the proper function of poesy for the
early Aufklärer?

Art, in general, was perceived as ars popularis, "die das
Ergetzen und die Verbesserung des grössern Haufens der Menschen
suchet" (CD, p. 59). In looking back upon history, both
Gottsched and Breitinger agreed that poesy had proven itself
throughout the ages as "eine Lehrerin der Weissheit und Tugend"
and "eine Förderin der menschlichen Glückseligkeit" (CD, p.
103) and that it was dedicated to the "Verehrung Gottes, zur
Besserung des Nebenmenschen, und zu einer unschuldigen
Aufmunterung und Belustigung des Gemüthes" (CD, p. 103). Poesy
was to contribute to the "Erleuchtung des Verstandes" and to
the "Besserung des Willens", upon which all human happiness
depended (CD, pp. 105-106). And its "letzte Absicht" was the
Erbauung[9] of man (CD, p. 104). Common to all of the early
Aufklärer, then, was the deep concern for what may legitimately
be termed the aesthetic education of man.

In light of Bodmer's statement, an _enlivening_ of man's sensibilities was needed in order to combat ennui and medio- crity. Man needed to be freed from "[dem] verdrüsslichen Zustand einer Bewegungs-leeren Stille" (CD, p. 85). And since "die Unruh und Bewegung der Gemüthes-Leidenschaften" was considered pleasurable to man (CD, p. 85), motion[10] was seen as the chief means in the combatting of mental stagnation and moral degeneration. If art was to be effective, it had to _move_ the beholder. Man thus became "die vornehmste und wichtigste Materie vor die Poesie" (CD, p. 282).

The artist _alone_ was able to give "ein neues Ansehen" to common, ordinary and everyday occurrences and through the transformation of the real into the possible instill in man a renewed sense of life and vitality. Indeed, the true dignity and value of man was understood as residing in the powers of his own soul (CAW, p. 9). The key to the aesthetic education of man thus lay in the "Erregung der Leidenschaften" (J. E. Schlegel)[11]. This thought was also central to Baumgarten's aesthetics, wherein the arousal of strong emotions is under- stood as essential to an effective poetry: "Daher ist es ganz besonders poetisch, recht starke Affekte zu erregen" (Med. Para. 27, p. 115).

But how was the aesthetic education of man to be actualized?

The stirring of the emotions was to be accomplished both by means of lively imitation and the igniting of imagination in the creation of vibrant poetic images. Naturalness of expres- sion was equated, particularly in poetry, with liveliness of

imagery. The true strength and beauty of poesy was seen
as residing in the artistic unity of the possible with the new
and the marvelous. At the same time, however, literature had
to guard against being either too marvelous or too probable.
For whereas the former would cause a lack of interest, the
latter would stifle the excitement of art. The true art of
poesy thus consisted in the delicate balance between creative
imagination and imitation of nature.

Prevalent among the early Aufklärer was the idea that
tragedy, more strikingly than any other genre, was capable of
arousing "das erbauliche Ergetzen" (CD, p. 87). [emphasis mine]
Breitinger's statement is representative:

> Ja ich darf behaupten, dass so gar unter den
> bewegenden Stücken dijenigen die kräftigste
> Würckung haben, und das strengste Ergetzen
> gewähren, welche die heftigsten, ungestümsten
> und widerwärtigsten Gemüths-Leidenschaften,
> als Furcht, Schrecken, Mitleiden, erregen,
> weil die Kunst der Nachahmung diese Leiden-
> schaften...von allem würcklich Widerwärtigen
> reiniget; daher auch die Tragödie stärker
> anziehet und beweget als die Comödie (CD,
> pp. 86-87).

Thus aesthetic education consists in the purification of
excessive emotions, a purifying then of all vexatious inclination and offensiveness.

Although the experience of beauty also assisted in this
task by encouraging the avoidance of excess through the reflection of symmetry, order and perfection, it was really in
experiencing the sublime that man could gain a new appreciation
of his own capabilities and thus come to a fuller understanding

of his real potential in life. Through those "Einbildungen
von unserer Würde", experienced in moments of sublimity, the
spirit of man could be elevated to new heights of self-aware-
ness and thereby gain a new sense of personal dignity and worth.

The early Aufklärer thus believed that "garstige Lüste"
had no place in an art which sought "reines Ergetzen" (CD,
p. 75). In experiencing a perfect work of art, man comes to a
recognition of the "Schande des Lasters" (CD, p. 284). Man's
sense for the True, the Good and the Beautiful is gradually refined, in proportion with the degree to which unfavorable
emotions are purified of their vulgarity. Man's sensibilities
are thus spiritualized. Literature, then, was understood as
a vital form of art because of its wholesome contribution to
the edification and ennobling of man.

We set out to demonstrate and, in turn, have shown how
truly significant the many contributions to the poetics and
aesthetics of the early Aufklärung actually were for the
development of a genuinely national German literature. This
desire for independence and autonomy was perhaps best expressed
in the Bemühungen zur Beförderung der Critik und des guten
Geschmacks (1743/1744), wherein J. A. Cramer and C. Mylius
maintained that the German language was indeed rich enough to
produce good literature, but that this potential had simply
not been realized to its fullest.

> Doch es wird eine Zeit in Deutschland kommen,
> da seine Ehre als ein hellglänzendes Licht
> schimmern wird, weil seine Schriftsteller

> die Künste und Wissenschaften in der
> Muttersprache lehren werden: die Deutschen
> werden nicht mehr zu den Ausländern wallen
> dürfen, klug und vernünftig zu werden: die
> Weissheit und die Künste werden in deutschen
> Kleidungen einher gehen, und die uns erst
> verachtet, werden unsre Sprache erlernen
> müssen, ihre Stimme zu hören" (BBC, I, 41).

The fact, however, that Germany in the course of those few
years of the early Aufklärung, had already made a momentous
beginning in the advancement of this ideal did not escape the
attention of such critics:

> Und wie glücklich haben unser unsterblicher
> Wolf in der Weltweisheit, die berühmtesten
> Kunstrichter unserer Zeit, Gottsched, Bodmer,
> Breitinger and andre den Anfang schon zu
> derselben gemacht! (BBC, I, 41) [emphasis mine]

The development of a new language, which was vital to the
unfolding of a national literature, can be detected already in
the writings of the early enlightened critics. Under the
obvious influence of Pietism, one began to speak of moving the
heart ("das Hertz rühren"), and of the artist as a Schöpfer,
who contributes to the Erbauung of man. Thus, a new vitality
was present everywhere. And within one decade, the ideal, as
expressed, particularly by Cramer and Mylius, would be
realized in the poetry of a Klopstock, in the prose of a Wieland, and in the drama of a Lessing.

In looking back on the German Baroque, the early Aufklärer
felt a warm kinship with Martin Opitz. Both his poetry and
poetology were heralded as significant contributions to the
cultivation of good Taste in Germany. But this affinity to
Opitz has much deeper roots. For Opitz, poesy was "eine

verborgene Theologie" and practically everything the early
Aufklärer praised seems to reflect their agreement with this
insight: Bodmer's defense of Milton's Paradise Lost,
Breitinger's call for the creation of new and even invisible
worlds, the wide-spread glorification of Klopstock's odes and
his Messias (1748 ff.), i.e. the resounding affirmation of the
metaphysical aspects of Reality; Bodmer's concept of the sublime
and its emphasis on transcendence in man's feeling of having
been united with the All; and, in the common concern among all
early Aufklärer for the edification of man. Herein, we find
the true beginning of the idea of the poet-priest which was
further developed by Lessing and advocates of Sturm und Drang
and which reached fruition in the minds of the German Romantics.

However, in their development of criticism as a science,
in their deep concern for linguistic purity and in their
accentuation of the creative potential which man himself
possessed, the early Aufklärer turned away from the German
Baroque and looked to the future.[12]

In retrospect, we stress two very important aspects of the
work of Gottsched, Bodmer, Breitinger, Johann Elias Schlegel
and others which were enlightening to later thinkers in
Germany's intellectual history.

First and foremost, their belief in man's ultimate perfectibility, in humanitas, unites the early Aufklärer with the
later Aufklärung (Lessing and Wieland), with Sturm und Drang
(particularly, Herder), with German classicism (Goethe and
Schiller), and with German romanticism (especially Friedrich

Schlegel).

Secondly, these early enlightened critics, well in advance of Mendelssohn, Lessing, Kant, and Schiller, recognized the importance of moving the beholder. For, as practically the entire 18th Century agreed, the impassioning of man was intrinsic to his overall edification.

However, where there is continuity between the early Aufklärung and subsequent developments in Germany's intellectual history, there are notable differences.

The most obvious difference lies in the distinctly normative nature of the poetic theory of the early Aufklärer over and against the psychological individualization of nature by representatives of Sturm und Drang and German Romanticism. For the poetic theory of the early Aufklärung is informed by the deduction that beauty consists in symmetry, order and proportion.

The historical relativism present particularly in Breitinger's Critische Dichtkunst does not assume the status of an independent aesthetic category as it does, for instance, in the "characteristic" art of the young Goethe. Even Bodmer's concept of the sublime still remains subservient to ethics and theology and thus is unable to be enjoyed for its own sake. And although the creative imagination was free to create new and marvelous worlds, it was to remain within the bounds of probability. The German Romantics were the first to appreciate the autonomous nature of the sublime and first allowed the creative imagination to transcend the limits of probability.

In the call for a balance between the imitation of nature and creative imagination, and in the deep concern for symmetry, order and proportion in the creation of beautiful works of art, the early Aufklärung may be seen as precursory to German Classicism. It is this balance which determines both the freedom and the limitations of art for the early Aufklärer.

NOTES

Introduction

[1]
John G. Robertson, Studies in the Genesis of Romantic Theory in the Eighteenth Century (Cambridge: Cambridge University Press, 1923), p. 291.

[2]
This drawing by Monsaiux is part of the collection of the Bibliothèque Nationale of Paris. A famous engraving based on the drawing is that of Pierre-Louis Baquoy.

[3]
Die Monadologie was written in 1714 and first published in German translation by H. Köhler in 1720. The original French edition did not appear until 1839. See: G. W. Leibniz. Monadologie. Translated, introduced and explained by Hermann Glockner. (Stuttgart: Reclam-Verlag, 2nd ed. 1970), p. 26f. (esp. paragraphs 60, 62-63). See also: Peter Hanns Reill, The German Enlightenment and the Rise of Historicism (Berkeley: University of California Press, 1975), p. 7, for a similar statement.
Even among the most stimulating historical accounts of the Enlightenment to date, the German Aufklärer are dismissed as "isolated, impotent, and almost wholly unpolitical". This indictment is made by Peter Gay, in: The Enlightenment. An Interpretation. Vol. I: The Rise of Modern Paganism (New York: Alfred A. Knopf, 1966), 4. Gay's conclusion is the result of his obvious preference for the Franco-British contribution to the European Enlightenment. That this assessment is partial to that country whose period of enlightenment was revolutionary in character becomes quite evident in his monograph: Age of Enlightenment (New York: Times Incorporated, 1966), pp. 142-143.

[4]
This trend has developed from the methodology of Geistesgeschichte which was prominent in the 1920's and 1930's. The tendency to dichotomize along sharply delineated lines is obvious from Wilhelm Dilthey's theory of the type. The presupposition that individual developments in the life of the spirit/mind (Geist) can only be comprehended from the point of view of the whole and not from the perspective of the law of cause and effect operative in nature informs practically all forms of Geistesgeschichte. For Dilthey's interpretation of the German Aufklärung, in particular, see: Wilhelm Dilthey, Studien zur Geschichte des deutschen Geistes, Vol. III of: W. Dilthey. Gesammelte Schriften (Leipzig: B.G. Teubner,

1927), esp. : "Die Weltanschauung der deutschen Aufklärung",
p. 142f., which is part of the essay: "Friedrich der Grosse und
die deutsche Aufklärung", pp. 81-205.
Although Hermann A. Korff, in Geist der Goethezeit (1923/
1953) (Darmstadt: Wissenschaftliche Buchgesellschaft, 1974),
insists that Sturm und Drang signaled a break with the Aufklärung,
he did not overlook the basic continuity between Aufklärung and
German classicism. Neither did he fail to point out some
commonality between German classicism and German romanticism. It
was Fritz Strich, in Deutsche Klassik und Romantik; oder
Vollendung und Unendlichkeit. Ein Vergleich. (Bern: Francke
Verlag, 1922), who interpreted German classicism and German
romanticism as antitheses.

5
John G. Robertson, Studies, op. cit.; Friedrich J.
Schneider, Die deutsche Dichtung der Aufklärungszeit (Stuttgart:
J. B. Metzlersche Verlagsbuchhandlung, 1948): "So wenig wie
Rokoko und Aufklärung unversöhnliche Gegensätze sind, da man
vielmehr mit Cysarz das literarische Rokoko als eine durch die
Aufklärung bewirkte Läuterung des Barockstils anzusehen hat...
so können auch Empfindsamkeit und Aufklärung einander in
wechselseitiger Anpassung überformen und durchdringen, weil die
eine ihre Wurzel in emotionalem, die andere aber in intellek-
tuellem Grunde hat, Herz und Vernunft aber, wie schon Schillers
'schöne Seele' lehrt, nicht immer feindliche Mächte bleiben
müssen" (pp. 34-35).

6
"Einleitung" to: Emil Ermatinger, Deutsche Kultur im
Zeitalter der Aufklärung (1935) (Frankfurt a.M.: Athenaíon,
1969). This renewed interest in the Enlightenment, as
Wandruszka points out, is perfectly understandable in light of
the devastation of two world wars. Going beyond this, however,
Wandruszka maintains that the social and technological problems
which we experience today have their roots in the emergence of
middle-class industrial society at the time of the European
Enlightenment.

7
Janine Buenzod, "De l'Aufklärung an Sturm und Drang:
continuité au rupture?", in: Studies on Voltaire and the 18th
Century, ed. T. Besterman. XXIV (1963), pp. 289-314.

8
"Einleitung" to: Die Aufklärung. In ausgewählten Texten.
Ed. and intro. Gerhard Funke. (Stuttgart: K. F. Koehler Verlag,
1963).

9
Helmut Schanze, Romantik und Aufklärung. Untersuchungen
zu Friedrich Schlegel und Novalis (Nürnberg: Verlag Hans Carl,
1966).

10
    Georg Lukács, Skizze einer Geschichte der neueren deutschen Literatur (1953). We cite the 1963 edition (Neuwied: Luchterhand), p. 63. In his Goethe und seine Zeit (Bern: Francke Verlag, 1947), Lukács points tc the basic continuity between Aufklärung and German classicism. In this, there is basic agreement (although for different reasons) with Korff (see Note 4).

11
    Werner Krauss, Studien zur deutschen und französischen Aufklärung (Berlin: Rütten und Loening, 1963); and, W. K., Studien und Aufsätze (Berlin: Rütten und Loening, 1959). See also: Literaturgeschichte als geschichtlicher Auftrag. Werner Krauss zum 60. Geburstag. Ed. Werner Bahner. (Berlin: Rütten und Loening, 1961).

12
    Max Horkheimer/Theodor W. Adorno, Die Dialektik der Aufklärung. Philosophische Fragmente. (New York: Social Studies Assoc., Inc., 1944); (Frankfurt a.M.: S. Fischer Verlag, 1969).

13
    Peter Gay, The Enlightenment: An Interpretation, op. cit. This interpretation won the National Book Award in history for 1966.

14
    Peter Hanns Reill, The German Enlightenment and the Rise of Historicism, op. cit.

15
    Thomas Paine, The Age of Reason Being an Investigation of True and Fabulous Theology (Paris: Barrois, 1794).

16
    Latest interpretations of Enlightenment have focused upon the interaction of reason and emotion in the age. For instance: Robert Niklaus, in: A Literary History of France. The Eighteenth Century. 1715-1789 (London: Ernest Benn Limited, 1970), argues that the age of enlightenment is the age of reason and the age of sensibility in one (p. 389). He also maintains that Goethe's aphorism, "Avec Voltaire un siècle finit, avec Rousseau un siècle commence", can no longer be accepted (p. 390); Werner Bahner, "Aufklärung" als Perioden-begriff der Ideologiegeschichte (Berlin: Akademie Verlag, 1973); "Die Aufklärungsbewegung war in philosophischer Hinsicht nicht nur rationalistisch, sondern auch sensualistisch orientiert" (p. 13). See also: Irrationalism in the Eighteenth Century. Vol. II of: Studies in Eighteenth-Century Culture. Ed. Harold E. Pagliaro. (Cleveland/London: The Press of Case Western Reserve University, 1972). The investigation of the rational and irrational elements of Gotthold Ephraim Lessing's

thought is a primary undertaking of the Lessing Yearbook
(München: Max Hueber Verlag), the publication of the American
Lessing Society.

17   Although Leibniz maintains that ideas are innate to the
mind, the monad as such is characterized both in terms of
ideation and of striving. H. Glockner stresses that Leibniz
was as much a voluntarist as an intellectualist in his refresh-
ing introduction to Monadologie, op. cit., esp. p. 6. Glockner
concludes as follows: "Seine Weltanschauung ist vielmehr von
einem faustischen Streben getragen, das niemals völlig zum Ziele
gelangen kann" (p. 66).

18   As J. Minor points out, in: Fabeldichter, Satiriker
und Popularphilosophen des 18. Jahrhunderts (Berlin/Stuttgart:
W. Spemann) (Vol. 73 of Deutsche National-Litteratur. Ed.
Joseph Kürschner. Hereafter: DNL), Mendelssohn attempts to
mediate between the philosophical tenets of Leibniz and Wolff,
on the one hand, and Locke and Shaftesbury, on the other
(pp. 221-22).
     That Leibniz is the real father of the German Aufklärung
and that this period should be understood more in terms of
Leibniz than that of Descartes and Locke, see: Baron Cay von
Brockdorff, Die deutsche Aufklärungsphilosophie (Munchen:
Verlag Ernst Reinhardt, 1926); Fritz Brüggemann, "Einführung"
to: Das Weltbild der deutschen Aufklärung. Ed. F. B.
(Leipzig: Verlag von Philipp Reclam, 1930) (Vol. 2 of: Reihe
Aufklärung. Deutsche Literatur...in Entwicklungsreihen. Ed.
Heinz Kindermann. Hereafter: DLE); Ernst Cassirer, The
Philosophy of the Enlightenment. Trans. Fritz C. A. Koelln and
James P. Pettegrove (Princeton: Princeton University Press,
1951), esp. p. 299ff.; Hans M. Wolff disagrees and asserts
that the period must be understood in light of the accomplish-
ments of the "kleinere Denker", who he sees as the true
"Wegbereiter" of Auklärung, in: Die Weltanschauung der Aufklärung in geschichtlicher Entwicklung (Bern: Francke, 2nd
ed. 1963), p. 7.

19   In the Eighth Letter of Friedrich Schiller's Über die
ästhetische Erziehung in einer Reihe von Briefen (1795), we
find a call for the harmonization of "Vernunft" with "der
mutige Wille" and "das lebendige Gefühl". Friedrich Schiller.
Sämtliche Werke. Ed. Gerhard Fricke and Herbert Göpfert.
(München: Carl Hanser Verlag, 1967), Vol. V, 591. Concerning
the age of enlightenment, Schiller states: "...das Zeitalter
ist aufgeklärt, das heisst, die Kenntnisse sind gefunden und
öffentlich preisgegeben" (Werke V, 591). But man, in his
estimation, is not yet ripe (1795!) for true enlightenment.
This can only be achieved after the aesthetic education of man.
"Ausbildung des Empfindungsvermögens ist also das dringendere

Bedürfnis der Zeit", for "der Weg zu dem Kopf [muss] durch das Herz geöffnet werden" (Werke, V, 592). On the basis of this statement, rather late in the century, one may correctly perceive of the Aufklärung, as Kant did, as a movement.

20   Joseph Nadler, for instance, speaks of the "Kampf" between Aufklärung and pietism, in: J. N., Literaturgeschichte der deutschen Stämme und Landschaften. (Regensburg: Druck und Verlag von Josef Habbel, 1923), p. 392.

21   Gerhard Sauder, Empfindsamkeit (Stuttgart: J. B. Metzlersche Verlagsbuchhandlung, 1974): "Die Theoretiker der Empfindungen und der Empfindsamkeit wurden nicht müde, auf die Notwendigkeit einer Vereinigung von Vernunft und Gefühl, ein zu erstrebendes Gleichgewicht von Denken und Empfinden hinzuweisen" (p. 125).

22   As, for example, Friedrich Gundolf, Shakespeare und der deutsche Geist (Berlin: Georg Bondi, 1922). The extremism of his judgments with respect to the German Aufklärung is everywhere apparent. For instance: "Er [Gottsched] war der Genius des Rationalismus selbst und vollendete was Opitz nur begonnen: die Ausscheidung aller irrationalen Elemente zugunsten der erkennbaren Ordnung" (p. 91). Whereas Klopstock, Goethe, and George are seen as "Regeneratoren aus einem neuen Erleben", Opitz, Gottsched and Lessing "haben nichts Neues erlebt..." [!] (p. 59).

23   For an excellent discussion of Iselin's historical awareness, see: Peter Hanns Reill, The German Enlightenment and the Rise of Historicism, op. cit., p. 65ff.

24   Novalis [Friedrich von Hardenberg] , Die Christenheit oder Europa, in: Rowohlts Klassiker der Literatur und der Wissenschaft. Ed. Ernesto Grassi (Reinbek bei Hamburg: Rowohlt Taschenbuchverlag, 1963), Vol. XI: Novalis: "Nur Geduld, sie wird, sie muss kommen, die heilige Zeit des ewigen Friedens,..." (p. 52).

25   Lessings Werke. Ed. Kurt Wölfel. (Frankfurt a.M.: Insel Verlag, 1967), Vol. III: Schriften II, 561, Para. 85.

26   Christoph Martin Wieland, Geschichte des Agathon (1766/ 1767). Ed. Wolfgang Jahn. (München: Wilhelm Goldmann Verlag, 1965).

27   As Bildungsromane, Wieland's Agathon and Goethe's Wilhelm

Meisters Lehrjahre (1795/1796) are related not only in structure
and form, but also in the common development of their heroes
toward reconciliation and harmony with society. On this point,
however, Wieland's hero actually accomplishes this by the end of
the novel, where, with Goethe's Wilhelm Meister, we must assume
that he will eventually attain this harmony. The commonality of
the two novels, however, cannot be disputed.

28   In the words of Archytas, Agathon's spiritual father:
"...da wir nicht zweifeln dürfen, dass die undurchbrechbaren
Schranken unsrer Natur, auch bei der höchsten Anstrengung unsrer
Kraft, uns immer unendlich weit unter der wirklichen Vollkommen-
heit dieses Plans und seiner Ausführung zurück bleiben lassen"
(Geschichte des Agathon, op. cit., p. 527).

29   Johann Jacob Bodmer/ Johann Jacob Breitinger. Discourse
der Mahlern (1721-1723). Facsimile (Hildesheim/New York:
Georg Olms Verlagsbuchhandlung, 1969), XXI. Discours.

30   Johann Elias Schlegel, Der Fremde. Eine Wochenschrift.
(1745-1746), No. XLI, 18. Jan. 1746, in: Joh. Elias Schlegels
Werke. Ed. Johann Heinrich Schlegel (Copenhagen/Leipzig:
Christian Gottlob Prost und Rothens Erben, 1764ff.), Vol. V
(1770), 348. We cite the Herzog August Library (Wolfenbüttel)
edition.

31   Moses Mendelssohn's sämmtliche Werke. Ausgabe in Einem
Bande als National Denkmal (Wien: Mich. Schmidl's sel. Witwe
und Jg. Klang, 1838), Rhapsodie, oder Zusätze zu den Briefen
über die Empfindungen, p. 458. For similar statements, see:
pp. 455, 458, 459. Hereafter: Werke.

32   In: Friedrich Schiller. Sämtliche Werke. (München:
Carl Hanser Verlag, 4th ed., 1967), Ed. Gerhard Fricke and
Herbert G. Göpfert. p. 295.

33   Albrecht von Haller, Über den Ursprung des Übels, in:
Das Weltbild der deutschen Aufklärung, op. cit., p. 312.

34   Geschichte des Agathon, op. cit., p. 533.

35   Sämtliche Werke, op. cit., p. 296.

36   By aesthetics, we mean the study of beauty and the arts
as a branch of philosophy, following: Ruth Saw/Harold Osborn,
"Aesthetics as a Branch of Philosophy", British Journal of

Aesthetics, I, No. 1, p. 8ff. For Baumgarten, aesthetics was a philosophical discipline constituting the science of sensitive knowledge.

37
    In general: Hans Peter Herrmann, Naturnachahmung und Einbildungskraft. Zur Entwicklung der deutschen Poetik von 1670 bis 1740 (Bad Homburg: Gehlen, 1970); and, Karl-Heinz Stahl, Das Wunderbare als Problem und Gegenstand der deutschen Poetik des 17. und 18. Jahrhunderts (Frankfurt a.M.: Athenaïon, 1975). On Gottsched: Werner Rieck, Johann Christoph Gottsched. Eine kritische Würdigung seines Werkes (Berlin: Akademie-Verlag, 1972). On J. E. Schlegel: Elizabeth Wilkinson, Johann Elias Schlegel. A German Pioneer in Aesthetics (Oxford: Basil Blackwell, 1945).
    Herrmann's Habilitationsschrift is surely the most comprehensive, in-depth study of the poetics of the late Baroque and early Aufklärung in Germany to date. Although there is an advantage to first surveying the poetic theories of the Baroque before interpreting those of Aufklärung, such an approach is at the same time restrictive. This is particularly obvious in Herrmann's account of Gottsched. In his estimation, Gottsched's Critische Dichtkunst is in no way original, but rather "rückwärtsgewandt" (p. 276). Whereas Bodmer and Breitinger, for Herrmann, "stehen am Anfang der Aufklärung", Gottsched is placed within the period designation, "nachbarocke[r] Klassizismus" (p. 276). Herrmann continues: "Für Ursprünglichkeit jedoch hat Gottsched keinen Sinn" (p. 109); and, "Gottsched hat mit den Begriffen [elocutio, Witz, inventio, Naturnachahmung] in seiner Hand nichts anfangen können" (p. 161), etc. In all this, the echoes of previous scholars (ironically, the very ones against which Herrmann polemicizes in his introduction) are everywhere perceptible. See Note 42.

38
    Alfred Baeumler, Kants Kritik der Urteilskraft. Vol. I: Das Irrationalitätsproblem in der Ästhetik und Logik des 18. Jhs. bis zur Kritik der Urteilskraft. (Halle: Max Niemeyer, 1923).

39
    Christian Ludwig Liskow, "Vorrede" to: Carl Heinrich Heinekens Übertragung Dionysius Longin vom Erhabenen Griechisch und Teutsch (Dresden; 1742); Immanuel Pyra, Erweiss, dass die Gottschedianische Sekte den Geschmack verderbe/ Fortsetzung des Erweisses, dass... (1743/1744) Facsimile. (Hildesheim/New York: Georg Olms Verlagsbuchhandlung, 1974) Hereafter: EGS.; Georg Friedrich Meier, Beurtheilung der Gottschedischen Dichtkunst (1747) Facimile. (Hildesheim/New York: Georg Olms Verlag, 1975) Hereafter: BGD.

40
    In: Briefe, die neueste Litteratur betreffend. Ed. Friedrich Nicolai. (Berlin/Stettin: Nicolaïsche Buchhandlung,

3rd ed. 1767), pp. 97-107. For a thoughtful essay which calls
for an end to what is essentially name-calling with regard to
Gottsched's Circle, see: Robert R. Heitner, "A Gottschedian
Reply to Lessing's Seventeenth Literaturbrief", in: Studies
in Germanic Languages and Literatures. In Memory of Fred O.
Nolte. (St. Louis: Washington University Press, 1963), pp. 43-
58.

[41]   Johann Wolfgang Goethe, Dichtung und Wahrheit (Frankfurt
a.M.: Insel Verlag, 1975); "Für die Dichtkunst an und für sich
hatte man keinen Grundsatz finden können: sie war zu geistig
und flüchtig" (Vol. II, 294).

[42]   Gottsched, for example, is viewed as "der missverstandene
Leibniz" by Nadler, Literaturgeschichte, op. cit.; Friedrich
Braitmeier: "Er [Gottsched] hat von dem Wesen und Werden, von
der geschichtlichen Entwicklung weder der Sprache noch der Poesie
oder der Litteratur überhaupt je eine Ahnung gehabt, und so
meint er denn auch, auf dem Gebiet der Kunst lasse sich alles
nach Rezept und Schablone, machen", F. B. Geschichte der
Poetischen Theorie und Kritik von den Diskursen der Maler bis auf
Lessing. (Frauenfeld: J. Hubers Verlag, 2 Vols., 1888).
Köster points to Gottsched's lack of creativity, Albert Köster,
Die deutsche Literatur der Aufklärungszeit (Heidelberg: Carl
Winter Verlag, 1925); Newald does the same, Richard Newald,
Die deutsche Literatur vom Späthumanismus zur Empfindsamkeit
1570-1750 (München: C. H. Beck'sche Verlagsbuchhandlung, 1951);
Birke maintains "daß Gottsched ganz bei Wolff beruhigte und
keinen Ehrgeiz hatte, über ihn hinauszukommen", in: Joachim
Birke, Christian Wolffs Metaphysik und die zeitgenössische
Literatur- und Musiktheorie: Gottsched, Scheibe, Mizler
(Berlin: Walter de Gruyter, 1966); Gottsched's apologist is
Theodor W. Danzel, Gottsched und seine Zeit (Leipzig: Verlag
der Dyk'schen Buchhandlung, 1855). See also: Notes 22 and 37.

[43]   Johann Jacob Bodmer, Critische Betrachtungen über die
Poetischen Gemählde Der Dichter. Mit einer Vorrede von Johann
Jacob Breitinger. (Zürich: Orell/Leipzig: Gleditsch, 1741),
p. 1*. We cite a microfilmed copy of the Jantz Collection.
Hereafter: BPG.

[44]   See also: The "Einleitung" to Johann Christoph Gottsched'
Versuch einer Critischen Dichtkunst vor die Deutschen (Leipzig:
Breitkopf, 1730); Johann Jacob Bodmer, "Vorrede" to Johann Jacob
Breitinger's Critische Dichtkunst (Zürich: Orell, 1740); Georg
Friedrich Meier, "Eingang" to his Beurtheilung der Gottschedi-
schen Dichtkunst, op. cit.; and, Jakob Immanuel Pyra, Erweiss,
dass... op. cit., esp. "Von dem ersten Stücke".

[45]   Gerhard Funke, "Einleitung. Das sokratische Jahrhundert",

in: Die Aufklärung, op. cit., p. 90.

46   Renè Wellek, A History of Modern Criticism. Vol. I:
The Later 18th Century. (New Haven: Yale University Press,
1955).

47   We have anglicized the German word "Poetolog" as
poetologist, i.e. a theoretician of poesy. The same is true
of the words, poetology and poetological.

48   See: Paul Böckmann, Formgeschichte der deutschen Dichtung
(Hamburg: Hoffmann und Campe Verlag, 2 Vols., 1949).

NOTES

Chapter I

1   The full title of the first edition reads: Versuch
einer Critischen Dichtkunst vor die Deutschen;/Darinnen
erstlich die allgemeinen Regeln der Poesie,/hernach alle
besondere Gattungen der Gedichte,/abgehandelt und mit Exempeln
erläutert werden: Uberall aber gezeiget wird/Dass das innere
Wesen der Poesie/in einer Nachahmung der Natur/bestehe.
(Leipzig: Verlegts bey Bernhard Christoph Breitkopf, 1730).
We cite the University of Washington copy. All references to
this work are parenthetically inserted in the text as VCD.

2   See Rémy G. Saisselin, Taste in Eighteenth Century France.
Critical Reflections on the Origins of Aesthetics, or an
Apology for Amateurs (Syracuse: Syracuse University Press,
1965), p. 11, for a fresh appraisal of Boileau's poetics.

3   Bernhard Mencke was the founder of the Poetische
Gesellschaft (later, Deutsche Gesellschaft), whose Unterredung
von der Deutschen Poesie of 1710 had a profound effect on
Gottsched.

4   Hermann Hettner, Geschichte der deutschen Literatur im
achtzehnten Jahrhundert (Braunschweig: F. Vieweg und Sohn,
4. ed., 1893), Vol. I, 324. Hereafter cited as: Hettner.

5   Bruno Markwardt, Geschichte der deutschen Poetik. Vol.
II: Aufklärung, Rokoko, Sturm und Drang (Berlin: Walter de
Gruyter and Co., 1956), 67.

6   Hettner, Geschichte der deutschen Literatur, op. cit.,
p. 325.

7   As von Lempicki points out, Gottsched was actually quite
critical of Boileau. See: Sigmund von Lempicki, Geschichte
der deutschen Literaturwissenschaft bis zum Ende des 18.
Jahrhunderts (Göttingen: Vandenhoeck und Ruprecht, 2. ed.,
1968), p. 245.
    Walzel maintains that Le Bossu's Traité de Poëme épique
of 1675 had a greater influence on Gottsched than the L'Art
poétique of his teacher, Boileau. Oskar Walzel, Deutsche

Dichtung von Gottsched bis zur Gegenwart (Wildpark-Potsdam: Akademische Verlagsgesellschaft: Athenaion M.B.H., 1927), Vol. I, 38.

8   Rather than criticize Hettner from a perspective which varies in its basic presuppositions from those of the author (as Wilhelm Scherer did in his essay, "Hermann Hettners Litteraturgeschichte des 18. Jahrhunderts", in: *Kleine Schriften*, ed. by K. Burdach and E. Schmidt, Vol. II, Berlin, 1893, 66f.), we choose to meet him on his own ground and from there explore the merits of his research. Hettner's assessment of Gottsched's critical poetics, appearing at the end of German romanticism and at a time when empirical data was required of any scholarly research, fails, in this instance, to adhere to the principle that exact knowledge of sources constitutes objectivity in literary taxonomy.

9   In his major philosophical treatise, Gottsched maintains that the rules of the "freye Künste" are "gegründete Vorschriften von Verfertigung gewisser gelehrten Kunstwerke, darnach dieselben aufs geschickteste und vollkommenste eingerichtet werden können", *Erste Gründe der gesammten Weltweisheit* (1733) (Leipzig: Bernhard Christoph Breitkopf, 7. ed., 1762), p. 172. We cite the University of Washington copy (2 Vols.). All references to this work are parenthetically inserted in the text as *EGW*.

10   *Aristotle's Poetics*. Trans. by Leon Golden. (Englewood Cliffs: Prentice-Hall, Inc., 1968). Hereafter: *Poetics*.

11   It was Gottsched's contention that the ornamentation which he perceived in Hofmannswaldau's style was non-essential to a poetry whose main concern was for the effect it had upon the reader. Hofmannswaldau's excessive and weighty descriptions were seen as contributing to the loathsomeness which Gottsched despised, and his criticisms here are essentially the same as Boileau's misgivings with respect to Scuderi (see p. 3). The brunt of Gottsched's criticism, which has been overlooked, is concerned, not so much with the ornamental style of Marinism itself, but with its lack of excitement. "Eine lebhafte Beschreibung ist gut; aber lauter Bilder sind verdrüsslich zu lesen" (Translator's notes to Horace's *Ars poetica*, VCD, p. 11). Or: "Das ist der Fehler unsrer poetischen Mahler. Sie mischen Himmel und Erden durcheinander und kein Ding behält seine Stelle...Das heist Fische in den Wald, und das Wild in die See mahlen" (*VCD*, p. 12).

12   To my knowledge, no critic has noted the significance of these explanatory notes for an interpretation of Gottsched's poetry. They go far beyond mere commentary.

13   Although Wolfgang Preisendanz has demonstrated the
similarity between Gottsched's use of the terms Nachahmung
and Erfindung with inventio and elocutio ("Mimesis und Poiesis
in der deutschen Dichtungstheorie des 18. Jahrhunderts", in:
Rezeption und Produktion zwischen 1570 und 1730. Festschrift
für Günther Weydt zum 65. Geburtstag. Ed. by Wolfdietrich
Rasch, Hans Geulen und Klaus Haberkamm. (Bern/München: Francke
Verlag, 1972), p. 541), the influence of the rhetorical tradition on Gottsched's poetics has been generally overlooked.

14   In his Versuch eines Vollständigen Grammatisch-
Kritischen Wörterbuches der hochdeutschen Mundart mit be-
ständiger Vergleichung der übringen Mundarten (Leipzig:
Christoph Breitkopf und Sohn, 1774), Johann Christoph Adelung
defines Affect as follows:
        "...vom lateinischen Affectus, ein hoher Grad
        der Begierde und des Abscheues, eine heftige
        Leidenschaft. Anm. Leidenschaft und Affect
        werden oft für gleichbedeutend gehalten.
        Eigentlich sind sie es nicht, sondern sie
        sind der Stärke nach unterschieden..." (I, 151).
Adelung goes on to note that the word Gemüthsbewegung is only
partially synonymous with Affect. We use the more general term,
emotion, to represent the German word. See also: Gottsched's
Weltweisheit, I, 543. We cite the Wolfenbüttel copy of
Adelung's critical dictionary.

15   In reference to Cicero in the commentary to the 132nd
verse of his translation, Gottsched notes the importance of
having experienced a given emotion before being able to arouse
it in others (VCD, p. 18).

16   Even Gerstenberg had to admit: "Ein Theater-Skribent,
der eine wohlgewählte und an sich selbst schon rührende Fabel
hat...hat schon mehr als die Hälfte seiner Arbeit vollendet";
Heinrich Wilhelm von Gerstenberg, Briefe über Merkwürdigkeiten
der Literatur, 8. Brief, in: Sturm und Drang, Kritische
Schriften. (Heidelberg: Verlag Lambert Schneider, 1963),
p. 31.

17   "Wenn die Fabel erdacht ist, alsdann sucht der Poet
in der Historie erst eine ähnliche Begebenheit, und giebt
seinen Personen die bekannten Nahmen aus derselben, damit
sie desto wahrscheinlicher werde. Das heist das Wahre mit
dem Falschen vermischen; wie Aristoteles in seiner Poesie
weitläuftig zeiget" (VCD, p. 23).

18   As perpetuated by Hettner: "Gottsched kennt keinen
Zweck der Dichtung als den Zweck der trockensten und absicht-

lichsten Lehrhaftigkeit", Hettner, Geschichte der deutschen Literatur, op. cit., p. 325.

[19] It is for this reason that we believe Joachim Birke's interpretation of Gottsched's Critische Dichtkunst, (which is understood solely from the perspective of Wolffian philosophy) to be misdirected. Birke even goes so far as to insist that Gottsched's knowledge of Aristotle and Horace was derived from Christian Wolff's understanding of them. This is quite unconvincing in light of Gottsched's own translation of and commentary on Horace's Ars poetica which prefaces his Critische Dichtkunst. Joachim Birke, Christian Wolffs Metaphysik, op. cit.,

[20] Martini Opitii. Buch von der deutschen Poeterey. Ed. by R. Alewyn and R. Gruenter. (Tübingen: Max Niemeyer, 1963), p. 11.

[21] Handlexicon oder kurzgefasstes Wörterbuch der schönen Wissenschaften und freyen Künste. Ed. by J. C. Gottsched. (Leipzig: Caspar Fritschische Handlung, 1760). We cite the Wolfenbüttel copy, p. 1153. Also cited by Werner Rieck, Johann Christoph Gottsched, op. cit., p. 167.

[22] Handlexicon, op. cit., p. 1143. See: "Nachahmung überhaupt".

[23] Albert Köster. Die deutsche Literatur der Aufklärungszeit, op. cit., p. 12.

[24] Hans M. Wolff, Die Weltanschauung der deutschen Aufklärung, op. cit., p. 159.

[25] Richard Newald, Die deutsche Literatur. Vom Späthumanismus zur Empfindsamkeit. 1570-1750, op. cit., p. 497.

[26] Joachim Birke, Christian Wolffs Metaphysik, op. cit., This attitude is understandable when we discover Birke's basic presupposition: "Die Vergötterung der Vernunft machte Gottsched blind für andere Aspekte der Kunst" (p. 45).

[27] Susi Bing, Die Naturnachahmungstheorie bei Gottsched und den Schweizern und ihre Beziehung zu der Dichtungstheorie der Zeit (Würzburg: Konrad Triltsch Verlag, 1934), Diss. Köln.

[28] Wolfgang Bender, "Nachwort" to: Johann Jacob Breitinger, Critische Dichtkunst. Facsimile Edition (Stuttgart: J. B.

Metzlersche Verlagsbuchhandlung, 1966).

29   Werner Rieck, Johann Christoph Gottsched...op. cit.,
p. 167.

30   Johann Jacob Breitinger, Critische Dichtkunst. Worinnen
die Poetische Mahlerey in Absicht auf die Erfindung Im Grunde
untersuchet und mit Beyspielen aus den berühmtesten Alten und
Neuern erläutert wird. Mit einer Vorrede eingeführet von
Johann Jacob Bodemer. (Zürich: bey Conrad Orell und Comp.,
1740; Leipzig: bey Joh. Fried. Gleditsch, 1740). We cite
the facsimile edition (Stuttgart: J. B. Metzlersche
Verlagsbuchhandlung, 1966, 2 Vols.) Hereafter: CD.

31   L'Abbé C. Batteux, Les Beaux Arts Réduits á un Même
Principe. (Paris: Durand, 1746), xxii-xxiii. (University of
Washington copy).

32   Poetics, Chaps. I-IV.

33   The Works of Horace. With English Notes, by the Rev.
A. J. Maclene. Revised and edited by Reginald H. Chase.
(Boston: Allyn and Bacon, 1856), p. 231. 333.

34   See: Footnote 4, p. 1 of our Introduction.

35   Noted by: Katharine Everett Gilbert and Helmut Kuhn,
A History of Esthetics, (New York: Dover Publications, Inc.,
1972), p. 386.

36   Joseph Addison, The Spectator. (London: Printed for
J. and R. Tonson in the Strand, 8 Vols., 1744). We cite the
University of Washington copy. For the new and the marvelous,
see: Vol. VI, No. 412, for Monday, June 23, p. 66f. F.
Servaes has noted the almost verbatum reception of key passages
by Dubos in Breitinger's work. Franz Servaes, Die Poetik
Gottscheds und der Schweizer, Vol. 60 of: Quellen und
Forschungen zur Sprach - und Culturgeschichte der germanischen
Völker (Strassburg/London: Karl J. Trübner Verlag, 1887).

37   L'Abbé Dubos, Reflexions Critiques sur la Poésie et sur
la Peinture, 2 Vols., (Paris, 1719), Vol. I, Part I, Secs. 1,
3. We cite the University of Washington copy.

38   Ludovico Antonio Muratori, Della Perfetta Poesia Italiana
(1706). Noted by: Wolfgang Bender, J. J. Bodmer und J. J.
Breitinger (Stuttgart: J. B. Metzlersche Verlagsbuchhandlung,
1973), p. 113.

[39] Klaus Dockhorn, Macht und Wirkung der Rhetorik (Bad Homburg/Berlin/Zürich: 1968), Vol. 2 of: Respublica Literaria. A recent collection of essays devoted to this topic is: Rhetorik. Beiträge zu ihrer Geschichte in Deutschland vom 16. -20. Jahrhundert. Ed. by Helmut Schanze. (Frankfurt a.M.: Athenaïon, 1974). See the "Einleitung des Herausgebers" for a detailed account of the secondary sources on the subject.

[40] Bruno Markwardt, Geschichte der deutschen Poetik, op. cit., p. 2f.

[41] Noted by Dockhorn, Macht und Wirkung der Rhetorik, op. cit., p. 69 (Footnote 63).

[42] Johann Jacob Bodmer, Critische Abhandlung Von dem Wunderbaren in der Poesie und dessen Verbindung mit dem Wahrscheinlichen In einer Vertheidigung des Gedichtes Joh. Miltons von dem verlohrenen Paradiese; Der beygefüget ist Joseph Addisons Abhandlung von den Schönheiten in demselben Gedichte. (Zürich: Verlegts Conrad Orell und Comp. 1740). We cite the facsimile edition (Stuttgart: J. B. Metzlersche Verlagsbuchhandlung, 1966), p. 10. Hereafter cited as CAW.

[43] This influence is noted, in part, by Dockhorn, Macht und Wirkung der Rhetorik--op. cit., p. 49. However, Dockhorn's statement that the irrational is the moving principle of the art of rhetoric receives some criticism from Marie Luise Linn, who is, nonetheless, tolerant of Dockhorn's somewhat one-sided emphasis on movere to the almost complete exclusion of docere. Marie Luise Linn, "A. G. Baumgartens Aesthetica und die antike Rhetorik", in: Rhetorik--op. cit., p. 121 (Footnote 62).

[44] Dockhorn, Macht und Wirkung der Rhetorik--op. cit., p. 57.

[45] Johann Jacob Bodmer, Neue Critische Briefe über gantz verschniedenen Sachen, von verschiedenen Verfassen (Zürich: Conrad Orell und Comp., 1749). We cite the Göttingen copy, p. 45f. Hereafter: CB.

[46] "Möglichkeit", containing its own 'truth', is equated with "Ordnung und Verknüpfung der Umstände" in Bodmer's Critische Abhandlung von dem Wunderbaren--op. cit., p. 18.

[47] See: Katharine Gilbert and Helmut Kuhn, A History of Esthetics,--op. cit., p. 293.

[48]   Johann Sulzer, Theorie der schönen Künste (1771-1774).
We cite the University of Washington copy of the
second edition in 4 Vols, Vol. III, p. 487. Hereafter cited
as TKW, followed by the appropriate volume and page number.

[49]   Johannes Crüger, "Einleitung" to: Joh. Christoph
Gottsched und die Schweizer J. J. Bodmer und J. J. Breitinger
(Berlin/Stuttgart: Verlag von W. Spemann, 1882). DNL, Vol. 42.
Susi Bing, Die Naturnachahmungstheorie bei Gottsched und
den Schweizern, op. cit.; Wolfgang Bender, "Nachwort" to:
Johann Jacob Breitinger, Critische Dichtkunst, op. cit.;
Wolfgang Preisendanz, "Mimesis und Poiesis", op. cit.

[50]   Gottsched: "Dieser Witz ist eine Gemüths-Krafft,
welche die Aehnlichkeit der Dinge leicht wahrnehmen, und also
eine Vergleichung zwischen ihnen anstellen kan. Sie setzet
die Scharfsinnigkeit zum Grunde..." (VCD, p. 86, also p. 122).
See also: Gottsched, Erste Gründe der gesammten Weltweisheit,
op. cit., pp. 490-491).
     Adelung: "3. In der engsten, jetzt noch allein üblichen
Bedeutung ist der Witz, das Vermögen der Seele, Ähnlichkeiten,
und besonders verborgene Ähnlichkeiten zu entdecken, so wie
Scharfsinn das Vermögen ist, verborgene Unterschiede aufzufinden."
Johann Christoph Adelung, Versuch eines Vollständigen Gramma-
tisch-Kritischen Wörterbuches, op. cit., V, 266.

[51]   This goes back to the Discourse der Mahlern (1721-1723):
"Die stärckste Passionen eines Menschen sind die Eigenliebe
und die Ehrbegierde." Die Discourse der Mahlern. Part I.
Facsimile Edition (Hildesheim: Georg Olms, 1969), XX. Discourse.

[52]   Select Translations from Scaliger's Poetics, Trans.
Frederick Padelford (New York: Henry Holt and Co., 1905),
Yale Studies in English, Vol. 26, esp. 8.

[53]   Written in 1741; first publ. 1745 in: Neue Beyträge
zum Vergnügen des Verstandes und Witzes. We consider it
first, although published after the larger essay, Abhandlung
von der Nachahmung, because of its earlier completion and
impact upon the larger essay. All references to this essay
are parenthetically inserted in the text as ANS and are taken
from the collection: Johann Elias Schlegels Aesthetische und
Dramaturgische Schriften, Ed. and Intro. by Johann von
Antoniewicz (Heilbronn: Verlag von Gebr. Henninger, 1887).

[54]   References to this work (publ. 1742) are inserted in
the text as AN and are taken from Antoniewicz's edition.

55
    This is so for "Stärkere Empfindungen sind von grösserer Klarheit und somit auch poetischer als weniger klare und schwache" (paragraph 27); Alexander Baumgarten, Meditationes Philosophicae de Nonnullis ad Poema, in: Albert Riemann, Die Aesthetik Alexander Gottlieb Baumgartens (Halle: Verlag von Max Niemeyer, 1928), p. 114.

56
    Antoniewicz edition, p. 12.

57
    Wolfgang Bender, J. J. Bodmer und J. J. Breitinger-- op. cit., p. 91.

58
    Friedrich Braitmeier's statement, then, "daß Schlegel's Nachahmungstheorie nichts als die Breitingerische Lehre von der abstractio imaginationis in der Form der Wolffischen Terminologie und Methode ist" (F. B., Geschichte der poetischen Theorie und Kritik, op. cit., p. 294) is unacceptable on the basis of this evidence.

59
    Quoted from: Wolfgang Preisendanz, "Zur Poetik der deutschen Romantik I: Die Abkehr vom Grundsatz der Natur- nachahmung", in: Die deutsche Romantik. Poetik, Formen und Motive. Ed. by Hans Steffen. (Göttingen: Vandenhoeck und Ruprecht, 2. ed. 1970), p. 60.

60
    From: Lenz's Anmerkungen übers Theater (1774). Jakob Michael Reinhold Lenz. Werke und Schriften I. Ed. by Britta Titel and Hellmut Hang (Stuttgart: Henry Goverts Verlag, 1966), 337.

61
    Wolfgang Preisendanz ("Die Abkehr vom Grundsatz der Naturnachahmung", op. cit., p. 73) sees in Jean Paul and A. W. Schlegel the German romantic break with the imitation theory of the 18th Century. It remains to be seen, however, to what extent this thought was realized in the poetic works of German romanticism.

NOTES

Chapter II

1   Johann Jacob Bodmer, Von dem Einfluss und Gebrauche der
Einbildungs-Krafft: Zur Ausbesserung des Geschmackes: Oder
Genaue Untersuchung Aller Arten Beschreibungen, Worinne die
ausserlesenste Stellen Der berühmtesten Poeten dieser Zeit
mit gründtlicher Freyheit beurtheilt werden. (Zürich, 1727).
    We cite the Niedersächsische Landesbibliothek-
Göttingen copy. Hereafter cited as VEK.

2   Wolfgang Bender perceives of Bodmer's concept of the
creative imagination as the "Fahigkeit, vergangene Eindrücke
zu reproduzieren" and denies that Bodmer understood the
imagination as constituting an "eigenberechtigte produktive
Kraft". Wolfgang Bender, J. J. Bodmer und J. J. Breitinger,
op. cit., p. 72. This is a common opinion among critics.

3   We include here an excerpt from Friedrich Rudolf von
Canitz's (1654-1699) "Klag-Ode über den Tod seiner ersten
Gemahlin":
        Soll ich meine Doris missen?
        Hat sie mir der Tod entrissen?
            Oder bringt die Phantasey
            Mir vielleicht ein Schrecken bey?
        Lebt sie? Nein, sie ist verschwunden;
        Meine Doris deckt ein Grab.
        Schneid, Verhängniss, meinen Stunden
            Ungesäumt den Faden ab!
        ...
        Was für Wellen und für Flammen
        Schlagen über mich zusammen!
            Unaussprechlicher Verlust,
            Wie beklemmst du meine Brust!
        ...
        Mit was lieblichem Bezeigen
        Gab sie sich mir gantz zu eigen!
            Und wie sehr war sie bemüht,
            Bis sie meine Neigung rieth.
        Alles das hab ich verlohren!
            Ach! wie werd ich Traurens voll!
        Hat mein Unstern sich verschworen,
            Dass ich sterbend leben soll?
        ...

From: Des Freyherrn von Cani[t]z Gedichte, Nebst dessen Leben,
und Einer Untersuchung Von dem guten Geschmack In der Dicht-
und Rede-Kunst, ausgefertiget von Johann Ulrich König (Leipzig/
Berlin: Ambrosius Handen, 1727), p. 309 ff. We cite the
Wolfenbüttel copy. Hereafter: UGG.

4
    Edward P. J. Corbett, Classical Rhetoric for the Modern
Student (New York: Oxford University Press, 1965), p. 559.

5
    Johann Jacob Bodmer, Anklagung Des verderbten Geschmackes,
Oder Critische Anmerkungen Über Den Hamburgischen Patrioten,
Und Die Hallischen Tadlerinnen (Frankfurt und Leipzig; 1728).
    We cite the Göttingen copy. Hereafter cited as AVG.

6
    We cannot agree with H. M. Wolff that Witz, for Gottsched,
constitutes "die eigentliche Quelle der Kunst". It is but one
part of a greater whole for Gottsched. Furthermore, the
intellectualization of art which Wolff attributes to Gottsched
is simply not born out by fact. In general, Wolff, as Joachim
Birke was to do later, ties Gottsched much too closely to the
philosophy of Chr. Wolff. Hans M. Wolff, Die Weltanschauung
der deutschen Aufklärung, op. cit., p. 157f.

7
    "Die Einbildungskraft ist bei ihm [Gottsched] nur die
Fähigkeit zur Reproduktion einzelner Begriffe an Hand einzelner
Ähnlichkeiten mit gegenwärtigen Empfindungen...", H. P.
Herrmann, Naturnachahmung und Einbildungs Kraft, op. cit.,
p. 108.

8
    For a comprehensive account of the concept of "das
Wunderbare" in the 17th and 18th centuries, see: Karl-Heinz
Stahl, Das Wunderbare als Problem und Gegenstand der deutschen
Poetik des 17. und 18. Jahrhunderts (Frankfurt: Athenaion,
1975).

9
    Johann Jacob Breitinger, Critische Abhandlung von der
Natur, den Absichten und dem Gebrauche der Gleichnisse. Mit
Beyspielen aus den Schriften der berühmtesten alten und neuen
Schribenten erläutert. Durch Johann Jacob Bodmer besorget und
zum Drucke befördert. (Zürich: Conrad Orell und Comp., 1740).
We cite the facsimile edition (J. B. Metzlersche Verlags-
buchhandlung, 1967), p. 6f.

10
    Quoted from the German translation of the Meditationes
Philosophicae de Nonnullis ad Poema Pertinentibus by Albert
Riemann, Die Aesthetik Alexander Gottlieb Baumgartens, op. cit.,
p. 122.

11   J. Crüger makes the following remark concerning
Breitinger's reasoning here:
> "Wie vag und nichtssagend ist doch solche Definition!
> All diese möglichen Welten kennen wir nicht und
> können uns keine Vorstellung von ihnen machen...".

In: Johannes Crüger, "Einleitung" to: Joh. Christoph
Gottsched und die Schweizer J. J. Bodmer und J. J. Breitinger,
Vol. 42: DNL. (Berlin/Stuttgart: W. Spemann Verlag). As I
understand this world, it is one wherein the "Schöpferkraft"
of all things resides. In a sense, then, it is a world of
pure potential which lies behind the material and within the
spiritual worlds. Furthermore, Leibniz makes a significant
statement concerning this problem in his essay "Über die
Freiheit":
> "...wenn gewisse Möglichkeiten niemals existieren,
> so sind auch die existierenden Dinge nicht immer
> schlechterdings notwendig, denn sonst wäre es
> unmöglich, dass an ihrer Stelle andre existierten,
> und es würde damit, was niemals existierte, auch
> unmöglich sein. Nun werden doch aber unleugbar
> manche Erdichtungen, wie wir sie in Romanen
> finden, an sich für möglich gehalten, obwohl sie
> in dieser bestimmten Reihe des Universums, die
> Gott erwählt hat, keinen Platz finden; wenn man
> sich nicht etwa vorstellen will, dass, bei der
> unermesslichen Ausdehnung des Raumes und der Zeit,
> irgendwo auch die dichterischen Gefilde existieren,
> in denen König Artus und Amadis von Gallien und
> der sagenhafte Dietrich von Bern ein wirkliches
> Dasein führen".

In: G. W. Leibniz. Hauptschriften zur Grundlegung der
Philosophie. Ed. by E. Cassirer. Trans. by A. Buchenau.
(Leipzig: Dürr'schen, 1906), Vol. II, 497-498.

12   Anthony Earl of Shaftesbury, Charackteristicks of Men,
Manners, Opinions, Times, etc. (1711). We cite the University
of Washington copy. (London, 1733), in 3 Vols. See: "Advice
to an Author", Vol. I, Part III, Sec. 3, 207.

13   The immense impact of Klopstock's poetry on the German
reading public is particularly evident in J. G. Hess's letter
to Bodmer, written in Altstetten on May 17, 1749. After
having read Klopstock's poetic letters and odes[!], Hess lauds
and magnifies this creative genius and begs to be introduced to
him.
> "Wie seine heilige Dichtkunst, so auch seine
> edle Freundschaft, seine redliche Tugend,
> seine erhabene Grosmuth, seine zärtlichen
> Liebesschmerzen selbst, kurz alles was ich
> i[t]zt von ihm weiss, macht mir ihn im

höchsten Grade liebens- und verehrungswürdig".
In: Briefe berühmter und edler Deutschen an Bodmer. Ed. by
Gotthold Friedrich Stäudlin (Stuttgart: Verlag der Gebrüder
Mäntler, 1794), p. 102. We cite the Wolfenbüttel copy.

[14]   In: Das Weltbild der deutschen Aufklärung, op. cit.,
p. 69.

[15]   On the basis of this evidence, J. Birke's statement
that Gottsched's concept of Einbildungskraft is taken "fast
wörtlich" from Wolff is simply too strong. Joachim Birke,
Christian Wolffs Metaphysik, op. cit., p. 46.

NOTES

Chapter III

[1] Des Freyherrn von Cani[t]z Gedichte, Nebst dessen Leben, und Einer Untersuchung Von dem guten Geschmack in der Dicht- und Rede-Kunst, ausgefertiget von Johann Ulrich König (Leipzig/ Berlin: Ambrosius Handen, 1727), p. 238 (footnote). We cite the Wolfenbüttel copy. Hereafter: UGG.

[2] Gottfried Wilhelm Leibniz, Ermahnung an die Deutschen/ Von deutscher Sprachpflege (Darmstadt: Wissenschaftliche Buchgesellschaft, 1967). Hereafter: VdS. This work was printed as the first contribution to the Third Stück (1732) of the Beyträge Zur Kritischen Historie Der Deutschen Sprache, Poesie und Beredsamkeit, ed. by Johann Christoph Gottsched (Leipzig: Bernhard Christoph Breitkopf, 1732ff.). We cite the Wolfenbüttel copy (Ko 164) in 8 Vols. Hereafter: BKH. For Leibniz's work, see: Vol. I, 369-411.

[3] For an in-depth study, see: Eric A. Blackall, The Emergence of German as a Literary Language, 1700-1775 (Cambridge: Cambridge University Press, 1959); German trans. by Metzler, 1966.

[4] In his essay, "Von der Wörter Ordnung überhaupt in der deutschen Sprache", Gottsched attempts, not very successfully I may add, to prove on the basis of syntax that the poetry of Lohenstein and Hofmannswaldau is inferior to that of Gryphius and Günther-- "wie sie sehr grosse Fehler wieder die gemeine Wortfügung begangen, und daher zärtlichen Ohren sehr harte vorkommen" (BKH, I, p. 182).

[5] John G. Robertson, Studies in the Genesis of Romantic Theory in the Eighteenth Century, op. cit., p. 259.

[6] Wolfgang Bender, J. J. Bodmer und J. J. Breitinger, op. cit., p. 25.

[7] Robertson, Studies, op. cit., p. 261.

[8] Johann Jakob Bodmer/Johann Jakob Breitinger. Der Mahler der Sitten. (Hildesheim: Georg Olms Verlag, 2 Vols., 1972).

9
According to Robertson, op. cit. and Bender, op. cit.

10
Benedetto Croce, "Introduction to the Aesthetics of the Eighteenth Century", in: Philosophy-Poetry-History. An Anthology of Essays by Benedetto Croce. Trans. and Intro. by Cecil Sprigge. (London: Oxford University Press, 1966), p. 451.

11
Croce, "Introduction to the Aesthetics of the Eighteenth Century", op. cit., p. 453.

12
Bender, J. J. Bodmer und J. J. Breitinger, op. cit., p. 28.

13
Bodmer's promise of four more parts to his work, including one on Taste (VEK, p. 14), never materialized. It seems that, although Bodmer was a prolific writer, he tended to promise more than he could deliver.

14
König was thoroughly knowledgable of the important treatises on Taste, particularly those of the French. Robertson maintains that König was "the first German to introduce DuBos to his countrymen, the first to quote Shaftesbury": Robertson, Studies, op. cit., p. 255.

15
Trans. and annotated by D. August Friedrich Müller in three parts in 1715.

16
Briefe berühmter und edler Deutschen an Bodmer, op. cit., pp. 245-246.

17
Since the fourth edition of the work is also available to us, we shall cite this copy. We are aware, however, of extensive changes already in the second and third editions. J. J. Gottsched, Versuch einer Critischen Dichtkunst durchgehends mit den Exempeln unserer besten Dichter erläutert (Leipzig: Bernhard Christoph Breitkopf, 1751). We cite the University of Washington copy.

18
Johann Jacob Bodmer, Neue Critische Breife über gantz verschiedene Sachen, von verschiedenen Verfassern. (Zürich: Conrad Orell und Comp., 1749). We cite the Göttingen copy, p. 45f. Hereafter: NCB.

19
In: Sturm und Drang. Kritische Schriften. (Heidelberg: Verlag Lambert Schneider, 1963), p. 606

[20]   Quoted from: Elizabeth Wilkinson, Johann Elias Schlegel. A German Pioneer in Aesthetics (Oxford: Basil Blackwell, 1945), p. 104. Wilkinson, however, makes no mention of this fact in her study.

[21]   Johann Jacob Bodmer, Critische Briefe. We cite the facsimile edition (Hildesheim: Georg Olms Verlag, 1969). Hereafter: CB.

[22]   In light of this open and deliberate negative criticism of the "ignorant masses", perhaps Nietzsche's reference to the "Feindschaft der Deutschen gegen die Aufklärung" in the Morgenröte takes on new meaning.

[23]   Friedrich Schiller. Sämtliche Werke. Ed. by Gerhard Fricke and Herbert G. Göpfert (München: Carl Hanser Verlag, 4. ed., 1967), Vol. V, 489.

[24]   Heinrich Füssli's concepts of the marvelous and the sublime in relation to that of Bodmer's is soundly discussed by Marilyn K. Torbruegge, "Johann Heinrich Füssli und 'Bodmer-Longinus'. Das Wunderbare und das Erhabene", DVjS (1972), Heft 1, pp. 161-185. Nowhere in her article, however, does Torbruegge suggest the possible influence of Bodmer's Third Critical Letter on Füssli. Surely, this contribution is Bodmer's best statement on the sublime.

[25]   Discussed by Ernst Cassirer, Leibniz' System in seinen wissenschaftlichen Grundlagen (Marburg, 1902).

[26]   Anthony Earl of Shaftesbury, Charackteristicks of Men, Manners, Opinions, Times, etc. (1711). We cite the University of Washington copy (London: 2nd ed., 1733) in 3 Vols. See: "Advice to an Author", Vol. I, Part III, Sec. 3, 336f.; Francis Hutcheson, An Inquiry Into the Original of Our Ideas of Beauty and Virtue; In Two Treatises (1725). We cite the facsimile of the 3rd edition of 1738. (Westmead, Eng.: Gregg International Publishers Limited, 1969). Sec. I, Par. 14, p. 12f.

[27]   For Hume's ideas on the same, see: Ernst Cassirer, The Philosophy of the Enlightenment, op. cit., p. 305f.

[28]   R. G. Saisselin, Taste in Eighteenth Century France, op. cit., p. 74.

29   Johann Christoph Gottsched, Auszug aus des Herrn
Batteux,...aus dem einzigen Grundsatze der Nachahmung hergeleitet. (Leipzig; 1754).

30   Johann Adolf Schlegel, Batteux,...Einschränkung der
Schönen Künste auf einen einzigen Grundsatz (Leipzig; 1759).

31   Immanuel Pyra, Erweiss, dass die Gottschedianische
Sekte den Geschmack verderbe (1743)/Fortsetzung des Erweisses,
dass... Facsimile (Hildesheim: Georg Olms Verlag, 1974).

32   Georg Friedrich Meier, Beurtheilung der Gottschedischen
Dichtkunst. We cite the facimile edition (Hildesheim: Georg
Olms Verlag, 1975). Hereafter: BGD.

33   R. G. Saisselin, Taste, op. cit., p. 124.

NOTES

Conclusion

[1]   E. Reichmann is correct, then, when he asserts that the avoidance of Übermass, of excess, is the central concern of indeed all Aufklärer prior to Kant. Eberhard Reichmann, Die Herrschaft der Zahl, op. cit.

[2]   Franz Servaes, Die Poetik Gottsched und die Schweizer, op. cit., p. 3.

[3]   Susi Bing, Die Naturnachahmungstheorie bei Gottsched und den Schweizern, op. cit., p. 25.

[4]   Alfred Baeumler, Kants Kritik der Urteilskraft, op. cit. Vol. I, 155.

[5]   The Works of Plato. Trans. into English with analyses and introduction by B. Jowett (New York: Tudor Publishing Co.), Vol. IV, 287.

[6]   See also: Wolfgang Preisendanz, "Mimesis und Poiesis", op. cit. for additional discussion of the relation between imitation and imagination for the early Aufklärer.

[7]   Johann Jacob Bodmer, Critische Betrachtungen über die Poetischen Gemählde Der Dichter. Mit einer Vorrede von Johann Jacob Breitinger. (Zürich: Orell/Leipzig: Gleditsch, 1741). We cite the microfilmed copy of the Jantz Collection. Hereafter: BPG.

[8]   Johann Andreas Cramer/Christlob Mylius, Bemühungen zur Beförderung der Critik und des guten Geschmacks (Halle: We cite the Wolfenbüttel copy. Hereafter: BBC.

[9]   The use of this word clearly reveals the influence of Pietism on the poetic theory of this time. See: August Langen, Der Wortschatz des deutschen Pietismus (Tübingen: Max Niemeyer Verlag, 1954), p. 36.

[10]   The idea of motion as being central to action was common to German philosophy (Wolff, Leibniz, and esp. Gottsched's

dissertation), to the aesthetics of Dubos in France, in the concept of movere in the rhetorical tradition and in Pietism (see: Langen, op. cit., p. 36).

[11]   "Gedanken zur Aufnahme des dänischen Theaters", In: Antoniewicz edition, p. 213.

[12]   In that Gottsched, in particular, was well aware that he was living in a transitional age, and in light of his encouragement of criticism in Germany, we cannot agree with H. Herrmann that Gottsched is the last representative of the German Baroque tradition. H. P. Herrmann, Naturnachahmungs-theorie und Einbildungskraft, op. cit., p. 276.

A SELECT BIBLIOGRAPHY

I. Primary Sources:

Adelung, Johann Christoph. Versuch eines Vollständigen
     Grammatisch-Kritischen Wörterbuches der Hochdeutschen
     Mundart mit beständiger Vergleichung der übrigen
     Mundarten, besonders aber der Oberdeutschen. 5 Vols.
     Leipzig: Bernhard Christoph Breitkopf und Sohn, 1774 ff.

Addison, Joseph. The Spectator (1711-1714). 8 Vols. London:
     Printed for J. and R. Tonson in the Strand, 1744.

Aristotle's Poetics. Trans. by Leon Golden. Commentary by
     O. B. Hardison, Jr. Englewood Cliffs: Prentice-Hall,
     1968.

Batteux, L'Abbé C. Less Beaux Arts Réduits á un Même Principe.
     Paris: Durand, 1746.

Baumgarten, Alexander. Meditationes Philosophicae de
     Nonnullis ad Poema (1735), in: Albert Riemann. Die
     Aesthetik Alexander Gottlieb Baumgarten. Halle: Max
     Niemeyer, 1928.

Bodmer, Johann Joacob/Breitinger, Johann Jacob. ed. Die
     Discourse der Mahlern. Zürich: Joseph Lindinner,
     1721-1723. Facsimile. Hildesheim/New York: Georg Olms
     Verlagsbuchhandlung, 1969.

_____, Von dem Einfluss und Gebrauche der Einbildungs-
     Krafft: Zur Ausbesserung des Geschmackes: Oder Genaue
     Untersuchung Aller Arten Beschreibungen, Worinne die
     ausserlesenste Stellen Der berühmtesten Poeten dieser
     Zeit mit gründtlicher Freyheit beurtheilt werden.
     Franckfurt/Leipzig, 1727.

_____, Anklagung Des verderbten Geschmackes, Oder
     Critische Anmerkungen Uber Den Hamburgischen Patrioten,
     Und Die Hallischen Tadlerinnen. Frankfurt/Leipzig, 1728.

_____, Brief-Wechsel Von der Natur Des Poetischen
     Geschmackes. Dazu kömmt eine Untersuchung Wie ferne das
     Erhabene im Trauerspiele Statt und Platz haben könne:
     Wie auch von der Poetischen Gerechtigkeit. Zürich:
     Conrad Orell und Comp., 1736.

_____, Critische Abhandlung von dem Wunderbaren in der Poesie und dessen Verbindung mit dem Wahrscheinlichen. In einer Vertheidigung des Gedichtes Joh. Miltons von dem verlohrnen Paradiese: Der beygefüget ist Joseph Addisons Abhandlung von den Schönheiten in demselben Gedichte. Zürich: Conrad Orell und Comp., 1740. Facsimile. Stuttgart: J. B. Metzlersche Verlagsbuchhandlung, 1966.

_____, Critische Betrachtungen über die Poetischen Gemählde. Zürich: Conrad Orell und Comp., 1741.

_____, Critische Briefe. Zürich, 1746. Facsimile. Hildesheim/New York: Georg Olms Verlag, 1969.

Bodmer, Johann Jacob/Breitinger, Johann Jacob, ed. Der Mahler der Sitten. 2 Vols. Zürich: Conrad Orell und Comp., 1746. Facsimile. Hildesheim/New York: Georg Olms Verlag, 1972.

Bodmer, Johann Jacob. Neue Critische Briefe über gantz verschiedene Sachen, von verschiedenen Verfassern. Zürich: Conrad Orell und Comp., 1749.

Briefe berühmter und edler Deutschen an Bodmer. Ed. Gotthold Friedrich Ständlin Stuttgart: Verlag der Gebrüder Mäntler, 1794.

Breitinger, Johann Jacob. Critische Abhandlung Von der Natur den Absichten und dem Gebrauche der Gleichnisse, Mit Beyspielen aus den Schriften der berühmtesten alten und neuen Scribenten erläutert. Durch Johann Jacob Bodmer besorget und zum Drucke befördert. Zürich: Conrad Orell und Comp., 1740. Facsimile. Stuttgart: J. B. Metzlersche Verlagsbuchhandlung, 1967.

_____, Critische Dichtkunst Worinnen die Poetische Mahlerey in Absicht auf die Erfindung Im Grunde untersuchet und mit Beyspielen aus den berühmtesten Alten und Neuern erläutert wird. Mit einer Vorrede eingeführet von Johann Jacob Bodemer. 2 Vols. Zürich: Conrad Orell und Comp., 1740. Facsimile. Stuttgart: J. B. Metzlersche Verlagsbuchhandlung, 1966.

_____, ed. Sammlung Critscher, Poetischer, und andrer geistvollen Schriften. Zürich: Conrad Orell und Comp., 1741-1744.

Cramer, Johann Andreas/Mylius, Christlob, ed. Bemühungen zur Beförderung der Critik und des guten Geschmacks. Halle: Carl Herrmann Hemmerde, 1743.

Dubos, L' Abbé. Reflexions Critiques sur la Poésie et sur la Peinture. 2 Vols. (1719). Utrecht: Etienne Neaulme, 1732.

Goethe, Johann Wolfgang. Dichtung und Wahrheit (1811/1814). Frankfurt a.M.: Insel Verlag, 1975.

Gottsched, Johann Christoph. Versuch einer Critischen Dichtkunst vor die Deutschen; Darinnen erstlich die allgemeinen Regeln der Poesie, hernach alle besondere Gattungen der Gedichte, abgehandelt und mit Exempeln erläutert werden: Uberall aber gezeiget wird Dass das innere Wesen der Poesie in einer Nachahmung der Natur bestehe. Anstatt einer Einleitung ist Horatii Dichtkunst in deutsche Versse übersetzt, und mit Anmerckungen erläutert von M. Joh. Christoph Gottsched. Leipzig: Bernhard Christoph Breitkopf, 1730 ff.

_____, Beyträge Zur Kritischen Historie Der Deutschen Sprache, Poesie und Beredsamkeit. Leipzig: Bernhard Christoph Breitkopf, 1732 ff.

_____, Erste Gründe der gesammten Weltweisheit (1734 ff.) Leipzig: Bernhard Christoph Breitkopf, 7. ed., 1762.

_____, Lob-und Gedächtnissrede auf den Vater der deutschen Dichtkunst, MARTIN OPITZEN von BOBERFELD, Nachdem selbiger vor hundert Jahren in Danzig Todes verblichen, zur Erneurung Seines Andenkens im Jahre 1739 den 20 August auf der philosophischen Catheder zu Leipzig gehalten von Johann Christoph Gottscheden, P.P.O. Leipzig: Bernhard Christoph Breitkopf, 1739.

_____, ed. Neuer Büchersaal der schönen Wissenschaften und freyen Künste. Leipzig: Bernhard Christoph Breitkopf, 1745 ff.

_____, Auszug aus des Herrn Batteux...aus dem einzigen Grundsatz der Nachahmung hergeleitet. Leipzig, 1754.

_____, Handlexikon oder Kurzgefasstes Wörterbuch der schönen Wissenschaften und freyen Künste. Zum Gebrauche der Liebhaber derselben. Leipzig: Caspar Fritschische Handlung, 1760.

Hutcheson, Francis. An Inquiry Into the Original of Our Ideas of Beauty and Virtue, In Two Treatises (1725). Facsimile, 3 ed. Westmead, Eng.: Gregg International Publishers Limited, 1969.

König, Johann Ulrich. Des Freyherrn von Cani[t]z Gedichte,

Nebst dessen Leben, und Einer Untersuchung Von dem guten Geschmack in der Dicht-und Rede-Kunst. Leipzig/Berlin: Ambrosius Handen, 1727. .

Leibniz, Gottfried Wilhelm. Ermahnung an die Deutschen/Von deutscher Sprachpflege. Darmstadt: Wissenschaftliche Buchgesellschaft, 1967.

_____, Monadologie (1714/1720). Trans., intro. and explained by Hermann Glockner. Stuttgart: Reclam-Verlag, 2 ed. 1970.

Lenz, Jakob Michael Reinhold. Anmerkungen übers Theater (1774). In: Werke und Schriften I. Ed. Britta Titel and Hellmut Hang. Stuttgart: Henry Goverts Verlag, 1966.

Lessing, Gotthold Ephraim. Werke. Ed. Kurt Wölfel. Vol. III: Schriften II. Frankfurt a.M.: Insel Verlag, 1967.

Liskow, Christian Ludwig. "Vorrede" to: Carl Heinrich Heinekens Übertragung Dionysius Longin vom Erhabenen Griechisch und Teutsch. Dresden, 1742.

Meier, Georg Friedrich. Beurtheilung der Gottschedischen Dichtkunst. (1747-49) Facsimile. Hildesheim/New York. Georg Olms Verlag, 1975.

Mendelssohn, Moses. Sämmtliche Werke. Ausgabe in einem Bande als National Denkmal. Wien: Mich. Schmidl's und Jg. Klang, 1838. Nicolai, Friedrich, ed. Briefe, die neueste Litteratur betreffend. Berlin/Stettin: Nicolaische Buchhandlung, 3 ed. 1767.

Novalis [von Hardenberg, Friedrich]. Die Christenheit oder Europa. In: Rowohlts Klassiker der Literatur und der Wissenschaft. Ed. Ernesto Grassi, Vol. XI: Novalis. Reinbek bei Hamburg: Rowohlt Taschenbuchverlag, 1963.

Opitz, Martin. Buch von der deutschen Poeterey. ed. Richard Alewyn and Rainer Gruenter. Tübingen: Max Niemeyer, 1963.

Paine, Thomas. The Age of Reason Being an Investigation of True and Fabulous Theology. Paris: Barrois, 1794.

Plato. Ion. In: The Works of Plato. Trans. B. Jewett. New York: Tudor Publishing Co.

Pyra, Jakob Immanuel. Erweis, dass die Gottschedianische Sekte den Geschmack Verderbe/Fortsetzung des Erweises (1743-1744) Facsimile. Hildeshelm/New York: Georg Olms Verlag, 1974.

Scaliger. Select Translations from Scaliger's Poetics. Trans. Frederick Padelford. New York: Henry Holt and Co., 1905.

Schiller, Friedrich. Sämtliche Werke, Ed. Gerhard Fricke and Herbert Göpfert. München: Carl Hauser Verlag, 1967.

Schlegel, Johann Adolf. Batteux...Einschränkung der Schönen Künste auf einen einzigen Grundsatz. Leipzig, 1759.

Schlegel, Johann Elias. Werke, Ed. Johann Heinrich Schlegel. Kopenhagen/Leipzig: Christian Gottlob Prost und Rothens Erben. 1766 ff.

_____. Aesthetische und Dramatische Schriften. Ed. Johann von Antoniewica. Vol. 26 of: Deutsche Litteratur-denkmale des 18. und 19. Jahrhunderts, 1881.

Shaftesbury, Anthony Earl of. Charackteristicks of Men, Manners, Opinions, Times, etc. (1711). 3 Vols. London, 1733.

Sulzer, Johann G. Allgemeine Theorie der schönen Künste, (1771-1774) 4 Vols. Leipzig: Weidmannsche Buchhandlung, 2 ed., 1792-1799.

von Gerstenberg, Heinrich Wilhelm. Briefe über Merkwürdig-keiten der Literatur, (1766-1767) In: Sturm und Drang. Kritische Schriften. Heidelberg: Verlag Lambert Schneider, 1963.

von Haller, Albrecht. Über den Ursprung des Übels (1734). In: Das Weltbild der deutschen Aufklärung. Ed. Fritz Brüggemann. Leipzig: Philipp Reclam Verlag, 1930.

Wieland, Christoph Martin. Geschichte des Agathon (1766/1767). Ed. Wolfgang Jahn. München: Wilhelm Goldmann Verlag, 1965.

Wolff, Christian. Vernünftige Gedanken von Gott, der Welt und der Seele des Menschen (1720). In: Das Weltbild der deutschen Aufklärung, Ed. Fritz Brüggemann. Leipzig: Philipp Reclam Verlag, 1930.

II. Secondary Sources:

A. Literary Histories:

Ermatinger, Emil. Dichtung und Geistesleben der
    Deutschen Schweiz. München: C. H. Beck, 1933.

Hettner, Hermann. Geschichte der deutschen Literatur im
    achtzehnten Jahrhundert. Braunschweig: F. Vieweg
    und Sohn, 4 ed., 1893.

Korff, Hermann August. Geist der Goethezeit (1923/1953)
    Darmstadt: Wissenschaftliche Buchgesellschaft, 1974.

Köster, Albert. Die deutsche Literatur der Aufklärungszeit.
    Heidelberg: Carl Winter, 1925.

Lukács, Georg. Skizze einer Geschichte der neueren
    deutschen Literatur (1953). Neuwied: Luchterhand, 1963.

Martini, Fritz. "Von der Aufklärung zum Sturm und Drang".
    In: Annalen der deutschen Literatur. Ed. H. O. Burger
    Stuttgart: J. B. Metzlersche Verlagsbuchhandlung, 1971.

Nadler, Josef. Literaturgeschichte der deutschen Stämme
    und Landschaften. Regensburg: Josef Habbel Verlag,
    1923.

Newald, Richard. Die deutsche Literatur. Vom Späthumanismus
    zur Empfindsamkeit. 1570-1750. München: C. H.
    Beck'sche Verlagsbuchhandlung, 1951.

Niklaus, Robert. A Literary History of France. The
    Eighteenth Century. 1715-1789. London: Ernest Benn
    Limited, 1970.

Schneider, Friedrich J. Die deutsche Dichtung der
    Aufklärungszeit. Stuttgart: J. B. Metzlersche
    Verlagsbuchhandlung, 1948.

Viëtor, Karl. Das deutsche Dichten und Denken von der
    Aufklärung bis zum Realismus: Deutsche Literaturgeschichte
    von 1700 bis 1890. Berlin: Walter de Gruyter Verlag,
    3 ed., 1958.

Walzel, Oskar. Die deutsche Dichtung von Gottsched
    bis zur Gegenwart. Wildpart-Potsdam: Akademische
    Verlagsgesellschaft, 1927.

Wolff, Hans M. Die Weltanschauung der deutschen Aufklärung
    in geschichtlicher Entwicklung. Bern: Francke Verlag,
    1949.

B. Philosophical Works:

Baeumler, Alfred. Kants Kritik der Urteilskraft, ihre
    Geschichte und Systematik. Vol. I: Das Irrationalitäts-
    problem in der Ästhetik und Logik des 18. Jahrhunderts
    bis zur Kritik der Urteilskraft. Halle: Max Niemeyer,
    1923.

Brockdorff, Baron Cay von. Die deutsche Aufklärungs-
    philosophie. München: Verlag Ernst Reinhardt, 1926.

Cassirer, Ernst. The Philosophy of the Enlightenment. Trans.
    by Fritz C. A. Koelln and James P. Pettegrove.
    Princeton: Princeton University Press, 1951.

Copleston, Frederick. A History of Philosophy. Garden City:
    Image Books, Doubleday & Co. Inc. 1962.

Horkheimer, Max/Adorno, Theodor W. Die Dialektik der
    Aufklärung. Philosophische Fragmente. Frankfurt a.M.:
    S. Fischer Verlag, 1969.

C. Monographs:

Auerbach, Erich. Mimesis. Garden City: Doubleday, 1946.

Bahner, Werner. "Aufklärung" als Periodenbegriff der
    Ideologiegeschichte Berlin: Akademie Verlag, 1973.

Bing, Susi. Die Naturnachahmungstheorie bei Gottsched und
    den Schweizern und ihre Beziehung zu der Dichtungs-
    theorie der Zeit. Diss. Köln, Würzburg: Konrad
    Triltsch Verlag, 1934.

Birke, Joachim. Christian Wolffs Metaphysik und die
    zeitgenössische Literatur-und Musiktheorie:
    Gottsched, Scheibe, Mizler. Berlin: Walter de Gruyter
    Verlag, 1966.

Blackall, Eric A. The Emergence of German as a Literary
    Language. 1700-1775. Cambridge: Cambridge University
    Press, 1959.

Böckmann, Paul. Formgeschichte der deutschen Dichtung. 2 Vols. Hamburg: Hoffmann und Campe Verlag, 1949.

Corbett, Edward P. J. Classical Rhetoric for the Modern Student. New York: Oxford University Press, 1965.

Danzel, Theodor W. Gottsched und seine Zeit. Leipzig: Verlag der Dyk'schen Buchhandlung, 2nd ed., 1855.

Dilthey, Wilhelm. Studien zur Geschichte des deutschen Geistes (Leipzig: B. G. Teubner, 1927)

Dockhorn, Klaus. Macht und Wirkung der Rhetorik, Vol. 2. of: Respublica Literaria. Bad Homburg/Berlin/Zürich: Gehlen Verlag, 1968.

Gundolf, Friedrich. Shakespeare und der deutsche Geist. Berlin: Georg Bondi Verlag, 1922.

Herrmann, Hans Peter. Naturnachahmung und Einbildungskraft. Zur Entwicklung der deutschen Poetik von 1670 bis 1740. Bad Homburg: Gehlen, 1970.

Langen, August. Der Wortschatz des deutschen Pietismus. Tübingen: Max Niemeyer Verlag, 1954.

Lukács, Georg. Goethe und seine Zeit. Bern: Francke Verlag, 1947.

Martens, Wolfgang. Die Botschaft der Tugend. Die Aufklärung im Spiegel der deutschen moralischen Wochenschriften. Stuttgart: J. B. Metzlersche Verlagsbuchhandlung, 1968.

Rieck, Werner. Johann Christoph Gottsched. Eine Kritische Würdigung seines Werkes. Berlin: Akademie-Verlag, 1972.

Robertson, John G. Studies in the Genesis of Romantic Theory in the Eighteenth Century. Cambridge: Cambridge University Press, 1923.

Rosenthal, Bronislawa. Der Geniebegriff des Aufklärungs-zeitalters. Berlin: E. Ebering Verlag, 1933.

Saisselin, Rémy G. Taste in Eighteenth Century France. Syracuse: Syracuse University Press, 1965.

Sander, Gerhard. Empfindsamkeit. Stuttgart: J. B. Metzlersche Verlagsbuchhandlung, 1974.

Schanze, Helmut. Romantik und Aufklärung. Untersuchungen zu
    Friedrich Schlegel und Noralis. Nürnberg: Verlag
    Hans Carl, 1966.

Stahl, Karl-Heinz. Das Wunderbare als Problem und Gegenstand
    der deutschen Poetik des 17.und 18.Jahrhunderts.
    Frankfurt a.M.: Athenaion, 1975.

Strich, Fritz. Deutsche Klassik und Romantik; oder Vollendung
    und Unendlichkeit. Ein Vergleich. Bern: Francke Verlag,
    1962.

Krauss, Werner. Studien zur deutschen und französischen
    Aufklärung. Berlin: Rütten und Loening, 1963.

Unger, Rudolf. Hamann und die Aufklärung. Halle: Max
    Niemeyer Verlag, 1925.

Wehrli, Max. Johann Jakob Bodmer und die Geschichte der
    Literatur. Vol. 27 of: Wege zur Dichtung.
    Franenfeld/Leipzig: Huber und Co. Aktiengesellschaft,
    1937.

Wilkinson, Elizabeth M. Johann Elias Schlegel. A German
    Pioneer in Aesthetics. Basil Blackwell: Oxford, 1945.

    D. Literary Criticism:

Borinski, Karl. Die Antike in Poetik und Kunsttheorie vom
    Ausgang des Klassischen Alterthums bis auf Goethe
    und Wilhelm von Humboldt. Leipzig: 1914-1923.

Braitmeier, Friedrich. Geschichte der poetischen Theorie und
    Kritik von den Diskursen der Maler bis auf Lessing,
    2 Vols. Franenfeld: J. Hubers Verlag, 1888.

Gilbert, Kathryn/Kuhn, Helmut. A History of Esthetics.
    New York: Dover Publications, Inc., 1953.

Lempicki, Sigmund von. Geschichte der deutschen
    Literaturwissenschaft bis zum Ende des 18 Jahrhunderts.
    Göttingen: Vandenhoeck und Ruprecht, 2 ed. 1968.

Markwardt, Bruno. Geschichte der deutschen Poetik. Vol. II:
    Aufklärung, Rokoko und Sturm und Drang. Berlin:
    Walter de Gruyter und Co., 1956.

Servaes, Franz. Die Poetik Gottscheds und die Schweizer.
    Quellen und Forschungen zur Sprach-und Culturgeschichte

der germanischen Völker, 60.   Strassburg/London:
Karl J. Trübner Verlag, 1887.

Wellek, René. A History of Modern Criticism. Vol. I:
The Later 18th Century. New Haven: Yale University
Press, 1955.

E. Articles:

Bender, Wolfgang. "Nachwort: to: J. J. Breitinger's
Critische Dichtkunst. Facsimile (1966).

Brown, Andrew. "John Locke's Essay and Bodmer and Breitinger"
MLQ 10 (1949).

Brüggemann, Fritz. "Einführung" to: Aus der Frühzeit der
deutschen Aufklärung. Vol. 1 of: Reihe Aufklärung.
Deutsche Literatur...in Entwicklungsreihen. Weimar/
Leipzig: Herm. Böhlaus Nachf., 1928.

_____. "Einführung" to: Das Weltbild der deutschen
Aufklärung. Vol. 2 of: Reihe Aufklärung. Deutsche
Literatur...in Entwicklungsreihen. Ed. Heinz Kindermann.
Leipzig: Philipp Reclam, 1930.

Buenzod, Janine. "De l'Aufklärung an Sturm und Drang:
continuité au rupture?", in: Studies on Voltaire and
the 18th Century. Ed. T. Bestermann XXIV (1963), pp.
289-314.
Burger, Heinz Otto. "Deutsche Aufklärung im Widerspiel zu
Barock und Neubarock", in: Formkräfte der deutschen
Dichtung. Ed. Hans Steffen. Göttingen: Vandenhoeck
und Ruprecht, 1963, pp. 56-80.

Crüger, Johannes. "Einleitung" to: Johann Christoph
Gottsched und die Schweizer J. J. Bodmer und J. J.
Breitinger. Vol. 42 of: Deutsche National Litteratur.
Berlin/Stuttgart: W. Spemann Verlag.

Funke, Gerhard. "Einleitung. Das sokratische Jahrhundert",
in: Die Aufklärung. In ausgewählten Texten. Ed. G. F.
Stuttgart: K. F. Koehler Verlag, 1963.

Gaede, Friedrich. "Gottscheds Nachahmungstheorie und die Logik",
Deutsche Vierteljahresschrift für Literatur-und
Geistesgeschichte, Sonderheft, 1975, pp. 105*-117*.

Heitner, Robert. "A Gottschedian Reply to Lessing's
Seventeenth Literaturbrief", in: Studies in Germanic
Languages and Literatures. In Memory of Fred O. Nolte.

Ed. Erich Hofacker and Liselotte Dieckmann. St.
Louis: Washington University Press, 1963, pp. 43-58.

Minor, Jakob. "Einleitung" to: Fabeldichter, Satiriker und
Popularphilosophen des 18. Jahrhunderts. Vol. 73 of:
Deutsche National-Litteratur. Ed. Joseph Kürschner.
Berlin/Stuttgart: W. Spemann Verlag.

Osborn, Harold/Saw, Ruth. "Aesthetics as a Branch of Philosophy".
British Journal of Aesthetics I, No. 1, p. 8ff.

Preisendanz, Wolfgang. "Die Auseinandersetzung mit dem
Nachahmungsprinzip in Deutschland und die besondere Rolle
der Romane Wielands", in: Nachahmung und Illusion. Ed.
Hans R. Jauss, München: Eidos Verlag, 1964, pp. 72-95.

_____. "Mimesis und Poiesis in der deutschen
Dichtungstheorie des 18. Jahrhunderts". In: Rezeption
und Produktion zwischen 1570 und 1730. Festschrift für
Günther Weydt. Ed. Wolfdietrich Rasch, Hans Geulten and
Klaus Haberkamm. Bern/München: Francke Verlag, 1972.

Scherer, Wilhelm. "Hermann Hettners Litteraturgeschichte des
18. Jahrhunderts". In: W. S. Kleine Schriften. Ed.
K. Burdach and E. Schmidt. Berlin: Weidmannsche
Buchhandlung, 1893.

Torbruegge, Marilyn. "Johann Heinrich Füssli und Bodmer-
Longinus'. Das Wunderbare und das Erhabene". DVjS 46
(1972). pp. 161-85.

Viëtor, Karl. "Die Idee des Erhabenen in der deutschen
Literatur". in: Geist und Form. Bern: Francke, 1952.

Wandruszka, Adam. "Einleitung" to: Emil Ermatinger.
Deutsche Kultur im Zeitalter der Aufklärung (1935).
Frankfurt a.M.: Athenaion Verlag, 1969.

Windfuhr, Manfred. "Nachwort" to: J. J. Breitinger's
Critische Abhandlung von der Natur, den Absichten
und dem Gebrauche der Gleichnisse. Facsimile. (1967).

   F. Collected Essays:

Bahner, Werner, ed. Literaturgeschichte als geschichtlicher
Auftrag. Werner Krauss zum 60. Geburtstag. Berlin:
Rütten und Loening, 1961.

Krauss, Werner. Studien und Aufsätze. Berlin: Rütten und
Loening, 1959.

Pagliaro, Harold E., ed. Studies in Eighteenth-Century Culture. Vol. II: Irrationalism in the Eighteenth Century. Cleveland/London: The Press of Case Western Reserve University, 1972.

Schanze, Helmut, ed. Rhetorik. Beiträge zu ihrer Geschichte in Deutschland vom 16. - 20. Jahrhundert. Frankfurt a.M.: Athenaion Verlag, 1974.

G. General Histories:

Biedermann, Karl. Deutschland im 18. Jahrhundert. 5 Vols. Leipzig: J. J. Weber Verlag, 2 ed., 1880.

Bruford, W. H. Germany in the 18th Century: The Social Background of the Literary Revival, Cambridge: Cambridge Univ. Press, 1935.

Ermatinger, Emil. Deutsche Kultur im Zeitalter der Aufklärung. Frankfurt a.M.: Athenaion Verlag, 1969.

Gay, Peter. The Enlightenment: An Interpretation. Vol. I: The Rise of Modern Paganism. New York: Alfred A. Knopf, 1966.

Hazard, Paul. La Pensée européenne au 18 iéme siécle: de Montesquieu á Lessing, Paris: Boivin et cie, 1946.

Reill, Peter Hanns. The German Enlightment and the Rise of Historicism. Berkeley: University of California Press, 1975.

H. Bibliographical Sources:

Bender, Wolfgang. J. J. Bodmer und J. J. Breitinger. Stuttgart: J. B. Metzlersche Verlagsbuchhandlung, 1973.

Eppelsheimer, H. W./Köttelwesch, C., eds. Bibliographie der deutschen Literaturwissenschaft. 1959 ff.

Goede ke, Karl, ed. Grundriss zur Geschichte der deutschen Dichtung. 13. Vols., 1884-1953.

Grotegut, E. K./Leneaux, G. F. Das Zeitalter der Aufklärung. Vol. 6 of: Handbuch der deutschen Literaturgeschichte, 1974.

DATE DUE

WITHDRAWN